Stream and Gliding Sun
A Wicklow Anthology
Edited by David Wheatley

*'Through intricate motions ran
Stream and gliding sun...'*

W.B. Yeats, 'Stream and Sun at Glendalough'

Stream and Gliding Sun
A Wicklow Anthology

Edited by David Wheatley

First published in 1998 © Wicklow County Council
Produced by Wicklow County Council

ISBN 0-9533904-1-1

Wicklow County Council wishes to acknowledge assistance provided by Wicklow Rural Partnership Ltd. for this publication.

FOREWORD

It is my pleasure to introduce the publication of *Stream and Gliding Sun: A Wicklow Anthology,* edited by David Wheatley. This work has been made possible by the establishment of the Writer in Residence Programme co-ordinated by Wicklow County Council. I wish to congratulate David Wheatley, our Writer in Residence this year. He has provided us with a rich and colourful selection of writing for which we are grateful and certainly most proud. We are very priviledged to have such an impressive selection of writing from and about County Wicklow. As a local authority we are pleased to assist David's work and this his second publication. I am confident that Stream and Gliding Sun will provide many hours of pleasure and continue the important tradition of writing in County Wicklow.

Blaise Treacy
County Manager

On behalf of the members of Wicklow County Council I wish to congratulate the County Manager and the Arts Programme of Wicklow County Council for the initiative in undertaking a publication of this nature. I acknowledge the work and dedication of the Arts Section and the County Library Service in this initiative. *Stream and Gliding Sun* provides a fascinating selection of literature from so many great writers as well as providing a platform for many emerging writers. It is my hope that this publication will further assist the development of the arts in the county and provide much enjoyment for you the reader.

Cllr. Liam Kavanagh
Chairman Wicklow County Council

CONTENTS

Introduction   8

John Millington Synge	PRELUDE	11
Samuel Beckett	from MERCIER AND CAMIER	12
Thomas Moore	THE MEETING OF THE WATERS	13
Gerald of Wales	from THE HISTORY AND TOPOGRAPHY OF IRELAND	14
Sean O'Faolain	from A BROKEN WORLD	15
George Francis Savage-Armstrong	TO WICKLOW	20
Patrick Deeley	GLIMPSED THROUGH A CLEARING	22
	DARGLE OAK	22
	SPRIG OF SHILLELAGH	23
Jimmy Smullen	THE MEN OF THIRTY-SIX	24
F.R. Falkiner	GREYSTONES ROCKS	26
John Millington Synge	THE PEOPLE OF THE GLENS	27
	from THE TINKER'S WEDDING	34
Hugh Maxton	from WAKING	36
	YEATS AT GLENDALOUGH	39
W.B. Yeats	STREAM AND SUN AT GLENDALOUGH	41
Chevalier de la Tocnaye	from A FRENCHMAN'S WALK THROUGH IRELAND	42
J.B. Malone	from THE COMPLETE WICKLOW WAY	44
Seamus Heaney	ST KEVIN AND THE BLACKBIRD	48
Sir Walter Scott	A LETTER TO MARIA EDGEWORTH	49
William Drennan	from GLENDALLOCH	50
Donald Davie	THE PRIORY OF ST SAVIOUR, GLENDALOUGH	52
Derek Walcott	from OMEROS	53
Dave Smith	GLENDALOUGH'S ROUND TOWER	54
Harry Clifton	WINTER IN GLENMACNASS	55
Thomas Kinsella	KILLALANE	56
J.F. Lydon	from MEDIEVAL WICKLOW: 'A LAND OF WAR'	58
Mícheál Ó Cléirigh et al.	from THE ANNALS OF THE FOUR MASTERS	59
Aonghus MacDoighri Í Dhálaigh et al.	from THE BOOK OF THE O'BYRNES	62
J.P. McCall	MARCHING SONG OF FEAGH MACHUGH O'BYRNE	65
Joseph Holt	from THE LIFE AND ADVENTURES OF JOSEPH HOLT	67
Biddy Jenkinson	THE DESTRUCTION OF POETIC HABITAT	70
	CUAIRT AN CHLÁRAITHEORA AR GHLEANN DÁ LOCH	74
Luke Cullen	CROPPY BIDDY DOLAN	76
Anon.	DUNLAVIN GREEN	78
Mary Tighe	DWYER AND M'ALISTER	79
	LINES WRITTEN AT ROSSANA, NOVEMBER 18, 1799	83
Miles Byrne	from THE MEMOIRS OF MILES BYRNE	84
Anon.	BILLY BYRNE OF BALLYMANUS	86
Ethna Carbery	ANNE DEVLIN'S LAMENT FOR EMMET	88
John Millington Synge	QUEENS	89
	A QUESTION	90

William Blake	*from* JERUSALEM	91
Mark Granier	THE SUGARLOAF: LUNAR ECLIPSE WITH A COMET	92
Jonah Barrington	*from* PERSONAL SKETCHES AND RECOLLECTIONS	93
W.M. Thackeray	*from* THE IRISH SKETCH BOOK	96
Mr and Mrs Hall	*from* IRELAND, ITS SCENERY, CHARACTER &c.	98
Phil O'Keeffe	*from* STANDING AT THE CROSSROADS	100
Sylvia Bowe	STILL LIFE	103
Paul Durcan	LAMENT FOR CEARBHALL Ó DÁLAIGH	108
Fergus Allen	WALL OF DEATH, BRAY	111
Eilis Ní Dhuibhne	*from* THE BRAY HOUSE	112
Neil Jordan	*from* SUNRISE WITH SEA MONSTER	115
Caitríona O'Reilly	A WEEKEND IN BODEGA BAY	116
	EVENING, BRAY HARBOUR	116
	MICHELANGELO, THE CROUCHING BOY	117
	PERDITA	117
James McNeice	THE SWANS AT BRAY	118
Weston St John Joyce	*from* THE NEIGHBOURHOOD OF DUBLIN	119
Shane Harrison	SEE EMILY PLAY	121
Jerome O'Loughlin	NUMBER 15 USHER'S ISLAND	133
	YOU HAD NO BONE TO PICK,	
	SAM BECKETT, WITH GRAVEYARDS	133
John Millington Synge	THE OPPRESSION OF THE HILLS	134
	from THE SHADOW OF THE GLEN	138
Friedhelm Rathjen	SONG	139
Liz McManus	*from* ACTS OF SUBVERSION	140
Aidan Mathews	RETURNING TO KILCOOLE	141
Bill Tinley	*from* STRONGHOLDS: THREECASTLES	142
	GOLDEN HILL	143
	SMALL TALK	144
	A POSTCARD FROM TEGGIANO	145
Dennis O'Driscoll	POULAPHOUCA RESERVOIR	146
Michael Hamburger	*from* IRISH QUESTIONS	147
Elizabeth Smith	*from* THE WICKLOW WORLD OF ELIZABETH SMITH	149
Séamas Ó Maitiú and Barry O'Reilly	*from* BALLYKNOCKAN: A WICKLOW STONECUTTERS' VILLAGE	150
Anne Fitzgerald	RITUALS	151
	USES OF WATER	151
	BOUNDARIES OF A HINTERLAND	152
	EARLY ARRIVAL	152
Ninette de Valois	*from* COME DANCE WITH ME	153
Sebastian Barry	*from* THE STEWARD OF CHRISTENDOM	155
William Hanbidge	*from* THE MEMORIES OF WILLIAM HANBIDGE	157
Sylvester Gaffney	THE BATTLE OF BALTINGLASS	159
Áine Miller	INCIDENT AT THE SCALP	161
Austin Clarke	IN THE ROCKY GLEN	162

Nicola Lindsay	Haiku	164
	Can you not see?	165
	I'm not superstitious	165
Chevalier de la Tocnaye	*from* A Frenchman's Walk Through Ireland	166
Sheila Wingfield	Epiphany in a Country Church	167
Clemency Emmet	The White Room	168
Donald Davie	The Waterfall at Powerscourt	169
Carmen Cullen	Powerscourt Waterfall	170
	Bray Head	171
Roy McFadden	Enniskerry	172
Mary Lavin	*from* At Sallygap	173
Colum Kenny	Irish Breakfast	175
John Millington Synge	To the Oaks of Glencree	176
Weston St John Joyce	*from* The Neighbourhood of Dublin	177
David Wheatley	A Skimming Stone, Lough Bray	179
Standish O'Grady	Lough Bray	180
Breandán Breathnach	Piping in Wicklow	181
Anon.	The Cow Ate the Piper	183
Hugh Maxton	*from* Waking	185
Canon George Digby-Scott	*from* The Stones of Bray	187
Edward Byrne	*from* Parnell: A Memoir	188
Anon.	The Sweet Blackbird of Avondale	191
J F. Byrne	*from* Silent Years	193
John H. Edge	*from* An Irish Utopia	195
Richard Murphy	Roof-tree	197
John Montague	Luggala	198
Diarmaid Ó Muirithe	Some Wicklow Words	199
Marie O'Nolan	Sunday Lunch	200
Alma Brayden	DNA	207
	Early Walking	208
	Pacific in the Midlands	209
Jenny O'Donovan	Globular Fruit	210
Louise Tyner	Miracles	211
	Memories of the Theatre	213
Oscar Wilde	Requiescat	217
Christine Fuchs Gummpenberg	Glendalough	218
Seamus Heaney	A Norman Simile	219
Hugh Maxton	Waking	220
	Cloud	221
John Millington Synge	I've Thirty Months	222
	A Curse	222
Ludwig Wittgenstein	A Letter from Redcross	223
Charlotte Grace O'Brien	Wicklow	224
Anon.	On Deborah Perkins of the County of Wicklow	225

INTRODUCTION

ALTHOUGH WICKLOW WAS THE LAST of Ireland's 32 counties to be formed, it yields to few if any in the richness of its literary heritage. In *Stream and Gliding Sun* I have attempted to assemble a cross-section of writing from and about the county, in poetry and prose, by Irish and non-Irish writers alike, from earliest times to the present day. Visiting Wicklow in the twelfth century, Gerald of Wales found genetic mutations produced, he alleged, by the proclivity of the locals to bestiality. Later visitors were to be more charitable. The impressions of Le Chevalier de la Tocnaye, Thackeray, Donald Davie and Derek Walcott all testify to the physical beauty, inspiring antiquities and friendly populace of the county. Moving on to the Irish, the struggle was less to find which writers had Wicklow connections than to find which ones didn't—few enough, when one considers the extracts assembled here from William Drennan, Mary Tighe, Oscar Wilde, W.B. Yeats, Samuel Beckett, Austin Clarke, Sean O'Faolain, Mary Lavin, Thomas Kinsella, Seamus Heaney, Paul Durcan and Hugh Maxton. If not all Wicklowmen and women by birth, for the purposes of the present volume they are all Wicklowmen and women in the eyes of God. Pride of place, however, must go to the greatest literary Wicklowman of all, John Millington Synge. Other writers are represented by more than one extract, but none can match Synge for the depth of his devotion to the county and his unfailingly moving portrayals of it in his drama, poetry and essays.

Wicklow's connections with the rebellion of 1798 are marked in writings by and about such '98 notables as Joseph Holt, Michael Dwyer, Samuel McAllister, Miles Byrne, Anne Devlin and Biddy Dolan. The folk tradition is acknowledged in a selection of political and humorous ballads, including such favourites as 'Billy Byrne of Ballymanus', 'The Cow Ate the Piper' and 'The Battle of Baltinglass'. Miscellaneous items include a walk from J.B. Malone's *The Complete Wicklow Way*, a letter by the philosopher Ludwig Wittgenstein, a fourteenth-century Wicklow heretic, Adam Duff O'Toole, and an extract from William Blake's visionary poem *Jerusalem*. Finally, the anthology contains a generous selection of the writers, both previously published and unpublished, who attended my County Writers Group during my time as Wicklow County Writer in Residence from April to October 1998. *Stream and Gliding Sun* would make no sense if it did not reflect the immense variety of literary work being done in the county today, and it is a pleasure to include their work here.

I could easily have filled an anthology twice or three times the size of the present volume, and regret not having more space here for local history and longer prose extracts. *Stream and Gliding Sun* is in no sense a reference book; readers in search of such a volume are referred to Ken Hannigan and William Nolan's monumental *Wicklow: History & Society* (Geography Publication, 1994). But what it does contain is a lively selection from a great and continuing tradition. If it gives readers even a fraction of the pleasure it has given me to compile, *Stream and Gliding Sun* will have done its work.

David Wheatley, September 1998

JAMES JOYCE: A NOTE

Ireland's greatest modern writer, James Joyce, has many associations with County Wicklow, but unfortunately could not be included in this book for reasons beyond our control. Interested readers might like to consult pages 605–606 of the 1960 Faber and Faber edition of *Finnegans Wake* ('Yad... Yee') and page 11 of the 1960 Penguin edition of *A Portrait of the Artist as a Young Man* ('Once he had washed his hands in the lavatory of the Wicklow Hotel... Only louder'), both of which we had hoped to use. The editor regrets and apologizes to readers for their omission.

PRELUDE

John Millington Synge

Still south I went and west and south again,
Through Wicklow from the morning till the night,
And far from cities, and the sight of men,
Lived with the sunshine, and the moon's delight.

I knew the stars, the flowers, and the birds,
The grey and wintry sides of many glens,
And did but half remember human words,
In converse with the mountains, moors, and fens.

FROM MERCIER AND CAMIER

Samuel Beckett

A road still carriageable climbs over the high moorland. It cuts across vast turfbogs, a thousand feet above sea-level, two thousand if you prefer. It leads to nothing any more. A few ruined forts, a few ruined dwellings. The sea is not far, just visible beyond the valleys dipping eastward, pale plinth as pale as the pale wall of sky. Tarns lie hidden in the folds of the moor, invisible from the road, reached by faint paths, under high over-hanging crags. All seems flat, or gently undulating, and there at a stone's throw these high crags, all unsuspected by the wayfarer. Of granite what is more. In the west the chain is at its highest, its peaks exalt even the most downcast eyes, peaks commanding the vast champaign land, the celebrated pastures, the golden vale. Before the travellers, as far as eye can reach, the road winds on into the south, uphill, but imperceptibly. None ever pass this way but beauty-spot hogs and fanatical trampers. Under its heather mask the quag allures, with an allurement not all mortals can resist. Then it swallows them up or the mist comes down. The city is not far either, from certain points its lights can be seen by night, its light rather, and by day its haze. Even the piers of the harbour can be distinguished, on very clear days, of the two harbours, tiny arms in the glassy sea outflung, known flat, seen raised. And the islands and promontories, one has only to stop and turn at the right place, and of course by night the beacon lights, both flashing and revolving. It is here one would lie down, in a hollow bedded with dry heather, and fall asleep, for the last time, on an afternoon, in the sun, head down among the minute life of stems and bells, and fast fall asleep, fast farewell to charming things. It's a birdless sky, the odd raptor, no song. End of descriptive passage.

THE MEETING OF THE WATERS

Thomas Moore

There is not in the wide world a valley so sweet
As that vale in whose bosom the bright waters meet;
Oh! the last rays of feeling and life must depart,
Ere the bloom of that valley shall fade from my heart.

Yet it *was* not that Nature had shed o'er the scene
Her purest of crystal and brightest of green;
'Twas *not* her soft magic of streamlet or hill,
Oh! no,—it was something more exquisite still.

'Twas that friends, the belov'd of my bosom, were near,
Who made every dear scene of enchantment more dear,
And who felt how the best charms of nature improve,
When we see them reflected from looks that we love.

Sweet vale of Avoca! how calm would I rest
In thy bosom of shade, with the friends I love best,
Where the storms that we feel in this cold world should cease,
And our hearts, like thy waters, be mingled in peace.

FROM THE HISTORY AND TOPOGRAPHY OF IRELAND

Gerald of Wales

A man that was half an ox and an ox that was half a man.

In the neighbourhood of Wicklow at the time when Maurice fitzGerald got possession of that county and the castle, an extraordinary man was seen—if indeed it be right to call him a man. He had all the parts of the human body except the extremities which were those of an ox. From the joinings of the hands with the arms and the feet with the legs, he had hooves the same as an ox. He had no hair on his head, but was disfigured with baldness both in front and behind. Here and there he had a little down instead of hair. His eyes were huge and were like those of an ox both in colour, and in being round. His face was flat as far as his mouth. Instead of a nose he had two holes to act as nostrils, but no protuberance. He could not speak at all; he could only low. He attended the court of Maurice for a long time. He came to dinner every day and, using his cleft hooves as hands, placed in his mouth whatever was given to him to eat. The Irish natives of the place, because the youths of the castle often taunted them with begetting such beings on cows, secretly killed him in the end in envy and malice—a fate which he did not deserve.

Shortly before the coming of the English into the island a cow from a man's intercourse with her—a particular vice of that people—gave birth to a man-calf in the mountains around Glendalough. From this you may believe that once again a man that was half an ox, and an ox that was half a man was produced. It spent nearly a year with the other calves following its mother and feeding on her milk, and then, because it had more of the man than the beast, was transferred to the society of men.

Translated by John O'Meara

FROM A BROKEN WORLD

Sean O'Faolain

'Let me give you an example of what life is like in those isolated places,' jerking his head. 'When I was ordained my first parish was a lonely parish in the County Wicklow. From my presbytery window I could see the entire coast, a long straight beach, miles to the north, miles to the south, with a headland at each end stuck out into the sea. By the sea it is marsh. Then comes the first wave of high land around villages like Newtownmountkennedy. The land isn't bad on those hills, though it isn't what you would call really good land. They grow good turnips and potatoes and marigolds: the greens are not bad; but they cannot grow wheat. You need a good marl bottom for wheat. I was a young man then, and keen, so I studied these questions.'

(Whatever else you were, I said to myself, you must have been a bloody bore.)

'Look!' he said, pointing through the opposite window.

A vast, white plain, level as a sea, mapped with black hedgerows, all diminishing in size, spread away and away, maybe twenty miles, to a much lower range of mountains.

'My parish was in the same relation to that good land as these mountains here (nodding over his shoulder) in relation to that plain. That is to say, it was mountain bog, reclaimed by much labour, but always badly drained. Last of all, beyond me, was the utterly, miserably,'—his voice was almost oratorical here—'wretched moor. Miles and miles of it on the plateau of the mountain-tops. The native tribes lived as freebooters up there as late as the end of the eighteenth century. It was wooded then, and untouched by any road. Then, in Ninety-eight, two so-called Military Roads cut it across and across like a scissors. They were fifty miles long, and straight as rulers. By the way,' he asked suddenly, catching me looking idly out through the window, 'were you ever in County Wicklow?'

'Oh no, father,' I replied, as suddenly. I forced myself to attend. Just then my eyes caught the eye of an old farmer seated opposite me in the carriage; he was midway on the same seat as the priest, and, so, near enough to hear everything. A pool of water had gathered around each boot. Spits starred the dry patch between. Seeing me look at him he took from his mouth, with his entire fist, a bit of a cigarette he was smoking, and winked at me. Then he put back the cigarette and contemplated the priest's face with an air of childlike wonderment. At that wink I began to listen more carefully. Evidently my priest was a local 'character'.

'They are remarkable roads,' went on the priest. 'Well, the people of my parish were all poor. The interesting thing about them is that there were two sets of names—either the old tribal names, like O'Toole or O'Byrne or Doyle, or foreign names like Ryder, Nash, Greene, Pugh, Spink, Empie, Gascon, Latour.'

A little smile took the corners of his mouth as he said those names: but he never raised his eyes.

'The Greenes and Ryders and Pughs, and the rest of them, were soldiers who long ago trickled down into the houses of the poor, intermarried there, and became poor themselves as a result. However, they brought the people respect for law and order. Or; if you like, they knocked the last bit of rebel spirit out of them.'

'Interesting!' I said politely. I was beginning to enjoy the joke, for I could see the old farmer getting cross, and at the end of that last bit he had spat out his butt-end of cigarette.

'But the middle land, the good land, remained in the possession of the big people who never intermarried. When I went there to take over my duties I looked up the history of those wealthy people in *Debrett* and *Who's Who*, and *Burke's Landed Gentry*.'

His palm became an imaginary book, and with his pipe-stem he followed the lines and pretended to read:

'"Lord Blank, family name of Baron Blank. Fifth baron. Created in eighteen hundred and one. Lieutenant of the Seventeenth Hussars. Married Dorothy, oldest daughter of, let's say something like James Whipple Teaman of Grange House, Dilworth, Dorsetshire, you know the kind of thing. Succeeded his father in nineteen-eighteen. Educated at Eton and Sandhurst. Address, Grosvenor Square, London. Club—Travellers' or Brooks's. Recreations? Oh, as usual, hunting, shooting, fishing, racquets, riding."'

Again the thin-smile. The farmer was gob-open.

'My parishioners were their stable-boys, gate-lodge keepers, woodmen, beaters, farmhands, lady's-maids, etcetera. *They* were always intermarrying. *Their* bits of farms, reclaimed from the furze, were always being divided. I've seen people live on a bit of land about twice the size of this carriage.'

The farmer leaned forward, listening now with great interest. Our three heads nodded with the jolt of the train.

'Then there was emigration. In the five years I spent there I had one solitary marriage. I had sixty schoolchildren on roll when I went there. I had thirty-five when I left. Last year I heard they were reduced to eleven, and five of those were all one family. No wonder the county is full of ruins. You come on them in scores and scores, with, maybe, a tree growing out of the hearth, and the marks of the ridges they ploughed, still there, now smooth with grass.'

'Begobs, then, they're here too, father,' said the old farmer. The priest nodded sideways to him and proceeded:

'I liked the people. They were clean; hard-working; respectful. Too respectful—tipping their hats to everybody. They were always making what we call "the poor mouth"—a mendicant habit of centuries, I suppose. They gave me no trouble, except for two things. They had a habit of writing anonymous letters, and I couldn't stop it. They were at it all the time. They wrote them to one another.'

He paused. I prompted him. The farmer leaned closer and closer.

'The other thing?' I asked him.

'The other thing?' he said irritably to his pipe-bowl. 'In every one of these cabins they earned money by taking in boarded-out children—children unwanted by poor parents, or simply illegitimates. There was hardly a cottage without one, two, or three of these stranger children. They were well looked after, and the people often grew so fond of them they wouldn't part with them; and, I suppose, that was a nice trait too. But the point is that the only fresh blood coming into the county was… Well… a curious county, as you can see, and the morals were a bit curious too. However, that's enough said about them.'

And he had at least enough sense to go no further with that.

'Well, there you are. That was my parish, and you can't say it was a world in itself. It was too incomplete. Too many things left out. The human dignity of men is always impaired when, like that, they're depending on other people who can make or break them. They weren't men. They were servants. That's the whole of it.'

'But did that make their lives lonely? You said they were lonely?'

For the first time he looked up at me. The veins on his temples, swollen from holding his head down, throbbed with relief.

'I didn't say *they* were lonely.'

His eyes wavered sideways to the farmer. I easily followed him over the hiatus when he jumped to—

'One day, after three years without stepping out of my parish, I decided to see if the neighbouring parish was any better.' (When I heard the personal note come into his voice I wished the farmer was not there; as it was he kept to his cold, factual description.)

'Do you know, the contrast was amazing! When I climbed down to the valley and the good land! And it was the trees that made me realize it. Beeches instead of pines. Great, old beeches with roots like claws on the double ditches. The farm-houses too. They were large and prosperous with everything you might expect to find in a sturdy English farm—barns, ducks in the pond, thick-packed granaries, airy lofts, a pigeon-croft, a seat under an arbour, fruit-gardens.

'All that was good. But it was those beeches that really impressed me. They were so clean and old, not like the quick-growing pines of the mountains—dirty trees that scatter their needles into the shoots of the houses and block them up three times every winter.'

'Oh, they're buggurs, father!' agreed the farmer earnestly.

'I climbed lower still and came to the gates of the houses where the gentry used to live.'

'Used to?'

'Used to. I should have expected it, but somehow it hadn't occurred to me. It's funny how we all forget how time passes. But there they were—the gate-posts falling, The lodges boarded up. Notices, *For Sale*. Fifteen years of grass on the avenues. You see? "Owns ten thousand acres in Ireland. Address, Grosvenor Square, London."'

The pipe-stem travelled across the palm.

'I met an old man who took me down one of those avenues to see the ruins of a big house burned out during the troubled times. It was a lovely spring evening. The sky was like milk. The rooks were cawing about the roofless chimneys just like the flakes of soot come to life again. I spotted a queer little building at the end of a cypress avenue. The old man called it "the oftaphone." He meant octagon. It was a kind of peristyle. He said, "The Lord"—just like that, "The Lord used to have tea-parties and dances there long ago." I went into it and it had a magnificent view, a powerful view, across the valley over at my mountainy parish, yes, and beyond it to the ridges of the mountains, and even beyond that again to the very moors behind with their last little flecks and drifts of snow. They could have sat there and drunk their tea and seen my people—the poor Ryders, and Greenes, and O'Tooles, making little brown lines in the far-off fields in the ploughing time.'

'They could! Oh, begobs, father, so they could!'—and a mighty spit.

'Or at night, of summer evenings, they could have sipped their brandy and coffee and seen the little yellow lights of our cabin windows, and said, "How pretty it is!"'

'Begobs, yes! That's true!'

If anyone entered the carriage they he would have taken us for three friends, we were huddled together so eagerly. The priest went on:

'"They must have had good times here, once?" I said to the man who was with me. "The best, father!" says he. "Oh, the best out. The best while they lasted. And there were never any times like the old times. But they're scattered now, father," says he, "to the four winds. And they'll never come back." "Who owns the land, now?" I asked him. "They own it always, but who wants it?" says he, "The people here don't want it. They'd rather live in the towns and cities and work for wages."'

'That's right,' said the farmer, as if we were really discussing his own county, 'Begobs, you're talking sense now, father!'

'"The land was kept from them too long," says he. "And now they have lost the knack of it. I have two grown sons of my own," says he, "and they're after joining the British Army."'

'Begobs, yes!' said the farmer, leaning to catch every word; but the priest stopped, and leaned back.

The white, cold fields were singing by us. The cabins so still they might be rocks clung to the earth. The priest was looking at them and we were all looking at them, and at the flooded and frozen pools of water divided by the hedgerows. By his talk he had evoked a most powerful sense of comradeship in that carriage, whether he meant to or not: we felt one.

TO WICKLOW

George Francis Savage-Armstrong

'Tis not alone because amid thy woods,
   O Land of rest, or listening to thy streams,
Or loitering in thy rocky solitudes,
   I wander once again in happy dreams
With lost companions and vain Memory broods
   Amid the flickering leaves and dancing beams
On far off morns of mirth and boundless hopes,
That I revisit still thy well-loved slopes;

Not for this only; but that I once more
   Relive a cloudless boyhood on these hills,
And hear amid the waves upon thy shore
   And in the murmur of thy bounding rills
A voice that breathes a more than earthly lore,
   That holier passion here my bosom fills,
And nearer the fair unattainable
Clear heights of Perfect Life I seem to dwell.

Here Earth renews her freshness; unconfined
   The heavenward aspirations that have slept
Awake and soar; old habits of the mind
   Resume their joyful sway; the spirit that crept
With feeble foot, down-dropping, faint and blind,
   Forward once more on strenuous wing is swept;
Imagination's self is lithe and free
Between thy mountains and thy breaking sea.

There comes a quickening of the subtler sense
   Years and the world have deadened, that received
And gave into my being those intense
   And tremulous delights whereof bereaved
I languish in a darkness wide and dense,
   Delicate joys, faint sorrows, winds that heaved
The meadow-grass and shadows of the trees
Could move—vague fears, delicious ecstasies.

And once more—feebly, yet once more—I feel
   In Nature's deeps strange presences and powers,
And dim pulsations to my touch reveal
   The heart of things in lone and quiet hours;
Rare energies along my pulses steal;
   Fed with sweet air and dashed with freshening showers,
Like the bare leas when May hath touched the grass,
Into a golden summer life I pass.

Therefore for thy dear mountain-paths I sigh
   Even where the nightingales the livelong day
Warble beside Ilyssus, or the sky
   Bends o'er Rome's columns or Byzantium's bay;
Ay, yearn to make my dwelling where on high
   Slieve-Cullinn reddens in the morning ray,
Where wave the pines o'er Clara's bosky steep,
Or blithe Ovoca wanders to the deep.

THREE POEMS

Patrick Deeley

Glimpsed Through a Clearing

That bushy-bearded man must be
Charles Stewart Parnell
measuring half way up
the diameter of a larch at Avondale
(mast for a fishing vessel),
by means of a caliper—
which he himself has invented—
attached to a long pole.

Dargle Oak

A forgotten thermos flask,
stuck under the oxter
of the fallen oak. Which is
itself all but forgotten,

the god fallen, with one
intact arm jutting
out of this hillside. Root
below the mossy coverlet,

clay bark and mouldy wood
tuft to hand. A white grub
with an orange-capped head
plays dead. But here

is a sheltered surprise,
mere ghost of a green
chance, oak-leaf sprig-god,
redemptive, yet to rise.

SPRIG OF SHILLELAGH

Whoever gave the name *Sprig of Shillelagh*
to the last tree left standing
in all that old oak wood, may have been
laconic as any of those sturdy loners,
the timber-men, who had passed there before,
plodding and pulling their ponies
and their high carts, casting about them
a ship-oak eye. Or may have been
bombastic as Brousden, who found the wood
'so full of shades and wormholes…'

It scarcely makes a difference. The lovely
name-call spoken by the anonymous poet
soon belonged to all the people.
Whether there's a note of belittlement
in the title *Sprig*—a shred of lost glory
got at—and whether this was intended,
matters not. The ironmasters had
done their worst, hewn every coppice out,
corded and burned oak. The valleys
were branded by charcoal hearths, smelting

circles which to this day stand traceable.
The Sprig was already on its
last legs by 1830, and silence soon would tell
its story. Creatures it had fostered—
squirrels and birds—would have thinned
into defoliated distance. Only
the name, coming as a kind of corollary,
to one wistful onlooker, could linger
still about the tree, could embrace
it grown old or embrace it absent forever.

THE MEN OF THIRTY-SIX

Jimmy Smullen

(AIR: PADDY MCGINTY'S GOAT)

Scenery in Wicklow forever can be seen
But football All-Irelands are few and far between
In the year of thirty-six the only Junior one we won
To tell you all about it is a thing that can be done

Meath came a cropper in Navan one fine day
Next Carlow and the City Boys were sent upon their way
The Kildare and Cavan teams 'twas down they had to go
Now it's up to Dublin for the final against Mayo

There were bicycles and tricycles hitch-hikers by the score
The trams and the buses were packed right to the door
The taxi of the day was the family cart and ass
And the pipers playing music had come up from Baltinglass

Now Paddy McGinty a Wicklowman of note
In the pony and trap took along his famous goat
You couldn't get a ticket for this All-Ireland show
The day that County Wicklow played the County of Mayo.

The game had only started when Mayo shook the net
Mick Keating with all his brilliance a goal he had to get
But Wicklow hearts were saddened as the half-time whistle blew
It was Mayo well in front and the Wicklow scores too few

As the second half got on its way the air was full of gloom
Those Mayo lads were sending poor Wicklow to their gloom
It looked an easy title for the boys up from Mayo
But they forgot the fighting spirit of a man called Martin 'O'

He started with a point and his goal came roaring soon
Another point he shot over then Keating lowered the boom
You could hear all Wicklow cheering above and down below
The day that County Wicklow beat the county of Mayo

The moral of this story is that every team must have its day
It was those gallant sporting lads that won right through the fray
Excitement now all over and home they had to go
There was sunshine on the Wicklow hills and
Just moonlight in old Mayo.

GREYSTONES ROCKS

F.R. Falkiner

Even as these surges landward from the sea
    Do roll and swell and heave in vague emotion,
Then crash upon the coast in ecstasy
    The waters they have borne from far-off ocean—
So restless heave the depths of souls sublime
    With thoughts that came to them from realms eternal,
Till they burst, startling, on the coasts of time
    In passionate voices as of gods supernal.

And we who watch, as from a safe seashore,
    Could only, self-abash'd, look on in wonder
On things beyond our scope for evermore,
    As men of old might hear Olympian thunder,
But that the yearning of the heart within
Doth prove we, too, are of their God-like kin.

THE PEOPLE OF THE GLENS

John Millington Synge

Here and there in County Wicklow there are a number of little known places—places with curiously melodious names, such as Aughavanna, Glenmalure, Annamoe, or Lough Nahanagan—where the people have retained a peculiar simplicity, and speak a language in some ways more Elizabethan than the English of Connaught, where Irish was used till a much later date. In these glens many women still wear old-fashioned bonnets, with a frill round the face, and the old men, when they are going to the fair, or to Mass, are often seen in curiously-cut frock-coats, tall hats, and breeches buckled at the knee. When they meet a wanderer on foot, these old people are glad to stop and talk to him for hours, telling him stories of the Rebellion, or of the fallen angels that ride across the hills, or alluding to the three shadowy countries that are never forgotten in Wicklow—America (their El Dorado), the Union and the Madhouse.

'I had a power of children,' an old man who was born in Glenmalure, said to me once: 'I had a power of children, and they all went to California, with what I could give them, and bought a bit of a field. Then, when they put in the plough, it stuck fast on them. They looked in beneath it, and there was fine gold stretched within the earth. They're rich now and their daughters are riding on fine horses with new saddles on them, and elegant bits in their mouths, yet not a ha'porth did they ever send me, and may the devil ride with them to hell!'

Not long afterwards I met an old man wandering about a hill-side, where there was a fine view of Lough Dan, in extraordinary excitement and good spirits.

'I landed in Liverpool two days ago,' he said, when I had wished him the time of day; 'then I came to the city of Dublin this morning, and took the train to Bray, where you have the blue salt water on your left, and the beautiful valleys, with trees in them, on your right. From that I drove to this place on a jaunting-car to see some brothers and cousins I have living below. They're poor people, Mister, honey, with bits of cabins, and mud flows under them, but they're as happy as if they were in heaven, and what more could a man want than that? In America and Australia, and on the Atlantic Ocean, you have all sorts, good people and bad people, and murderers and thieves, and pickpockets; but in this place there isn't a being isn't as good and decent as yourself or me.'

I saw he was one of the old people one sometimes meets with who emigrated when the people were simpler than they are at present, and who often come back, after a lifetime in the States, as Irish as any old man who has never been twenty miles from the town of Wicklow. I asked him about his life abroad, when we had talked a little longer.

'I've been through perils enough to slay nations,' he said, 'and the people here think I should be rotten with gold, but they're better off the way they are. For five years I was a ship's smith, and never saw dry land, and I in all the danger and peril of the Atlantic Ocean. Then I was a veterinary surgeon, curing side-slip, splay-foot, spavin, splints, glanders, and the various ailments of the horse and ass. The lads in this place think you've nothing to do but to go across the sea and fill a bag with gold; but I tell you it is hard work, and in those countries the workhouses is full, and the prisons is full, and the crazyhouses is full, the same as in the city of Dublin. Over beyond you have fine dwellings, and you have only to put out your hand from the window among roses and vines, and the red wine grape; but there is all sorts in it, and the people is better in this country, among the trees and valleys, and they resting on their floors of mud.'

In Wicklow, as in the rest of Ireland, the Union, though it is a home of refuge for the tramps and tinkers, is looked on with supreme horror by the peasants. The madhouse, which they know better, is less dreaded.

One night I had to go down late in the evening from a mountain village to the town of Wicklow, and come back again into the hills. As soon as I came near Rathnew I passed many bands of girls and men making rather ruffianly flirtation on the pathway, and women who surged up to stare at me, as I passed in the middle of the road. The thick line of trees that are near Rathnew makes the way intensely dark, even on clear nights, and when one is riding quickly, the contrast, when one reaches the lights of Wicklow, is singularly abrupt. The town itself after nightfall is gloomy and squalid. Half-drunken men and women stand about, wrangling and disputing in the dull light from the windows, which is only strong enough to show the wretchedness of the figures which pass continually across them. I did my business quickly and turned back to the hills, passing for the first few miles the same noisy groups and couples on the roadway. After a while I stopped at a lonely public-house to get a drink and rest for a moment before I came to the hills. Six or seven men were talking drearily at one end of the room, and a woman I knew, who had been marketing in Wicklow, was resting nearer the door. When I had been given a glass of beer, I sat down on a barrel near her, and we began to talk.

'Ah, your honour,' she said, 'I hear you're going off in a short time to Dublin, or to France, and maybe we won't be in the place at all when you come back. There's no fences to the bit of farm I have, the way I'm destroyed running. The calves do be straying, and the geese do be straying, and the hens do be straying, and I'm destroyed running after them. We've no man in the place since himself died in the winter, and he ailing these five years, and there's no one to give us a hand drawing the hay or cutting the bit of oats we have above on the hill. My brother Michael has come back to his own place after being seven years in the Richmond Asylum; but what can you ask of him, and he with a long family of his own? And, indeed, it's a wonder he ever came back when it was a fine time he had in the asylum.'

She saw my movement of surprise, and went on:

'There was a son of my own, as fine a lad as you'd see in the county—though I'm his mother that says it, and you'd never think it to look at me. Well, he was a keeper in a kind of private asylum, I think they call it, and when Michael was taken bad, he went to see him, and didn't he know the keepers that were in charge of him, and they promised to take the best of care of him, and, indeed, he was always a quiet man that would give no trouble. After the first three years he was free in the place, and he walking about like a gentleman, doing any light work he'd find agreeable. Then my son went to see him a second time, and "You'll never see Michael again," says he when he came back, "for he's too well off where he is." And, indeed, it was well for him, but now he's come home.' Then she got up to carry out some groceries she was buying to the ass-cart that was waiting outside.

'It's really sorry I do be when I see you going off,' she said, as she was turning away. 'I don't often speak to you, but it's good company to see you passing up and down over the hill, and now may the Almighty God bless and preserve you, and see you safe home.'

A little later I was walking up the long hill which leads to the high ground from Laragh to Sugar Loaf. The solitude was intense. Towards the top of the hill I passed through a narrow gap with high rocks on one side of it and fir trees above them, and a handful of jagged sky filled with extraordinarily brilliant stars. In a few moments I passed out on the brow of the hill that runs behind the Devil's Glen, and smelt the fragrance of the bog. I mounted again. There was not light enough to show the mountains round me, and the earth seemed to have dwindled away into a mere platform where an astrologer might watch. Among these emotions of the night one cannot wonder that the madhouse is so often named in Wicklow.

Many of the old people of the country, however, when they have no definite sorrow, are not mournful, and are full of curious whims and observations. One old woman who lived near Glen Macnass told me that she had seen her sons had no hope of making a livelihood in the place where they were born, so, in addition to their schooling, she engaged a master to come over the bogs every evening and teach them sums and spelling. One evening she came in behind them, when they were at work and stopped to listen.

'And what do you think my son was after doing?' she said; 'he'd made a sum of how many times a wheel on a cart would turn round between the bridge below and the Post Office in Dublin. Would you believe that? I went out without saying a word, and I got the old stocking, where I kept a bit of money, and I made out what I owed the master. Then I went in again, and "Master," says I, "Mick's learning enough for the likes of him. You can go now and safe home to you." And, God bless you, Avourneen, Mick got a fine job after on the railroad.'

Another day, when she was trying to flatter me, she said: 'Ah, God bless you, Avourneen, you've no pride. Didn't I hear you yesterday, and you talking to my pig below in the field as if it was your brother? And a nice clean pig it is, too, the crathur.' A year or two afterwards I met this old woman again. Her husband had died a few months before of the 'Influence', and she was in pitiable distress, weeping and wailing while she talked to me. 'The poor old man is after dying on me,' she said, 'and he was great company. There's only one son left me now, and we do be killed working. Ah, Avourneen, the poor do have great stratagems to keep in their little cabins at all. And did you ever see the like of the place we live in? Isn't it the poorest, lonesomest, wildest, dreariest bit of a hill a person ever passed a life on?' When she stopped a moment, with the tears streaming on her face, I told a little about the poverty I had seen in Paris.

'God Almighty forgive me, Avourneen,' she went on, when I had finished, 'we don't know anything about it. We have our bit of turf, and our bit of sticks, and our bit to eat, and we have our health. Glory be to His Holy Name, not a one of the childer was ever a day ill, except one boy was hurted off a cart, and he never overed it. It's small right we have to complain at all.'

She died the following winter, and her son went to New York.

The old people who have direct tradition of the Rebellion, and a real interest in it, are growing less numerous daily, but one still meets with them here and there in the more remote districts.

One evening, at the beginning of harvest, as I was walking into a straggling village, far away in the mountains, in the southern half of the county, I overtook an old man walking in the same direction with an empty gallon can. I joined him; and when he had talked for a moment, he turned round and looked at me curiously.

'Begging your pardon, sir,' he said, 'I think you aren't Irish.' I told him he was mistaken.

'Well,' he went on, 'you don't speak the same as we do; so I was thinking maybe you were from another country.'

'I came back from France,' I said, 'two months ago, and maybe there's a trace of the language still upon my tongue.' He stopped and beamed with satisfaction.

'Ah,' he said, see that now. I knew there was something about you. I do be talking to all who do pass through this glen, telling them stories of the Rebellion, and the old histories of Ireland, and there's few can puzzle me, though I'm only a poor ignorant man.' He told me some of his adventures, and then he stopped again.

'Look at me now,' he said, 'and tell me what age you think I'd be.'

'You might be seventy,' I said.

'Ah,' he said, with a piteous whine in his voice, 'you wouldn't take me to be as old as that? No man ever thought me that age to this day.'

'Maybe you aren't far over sixty,' I said, fearing I had blundered; 'maybe you're sixty-four.' He beamed once more with delight, and hurried along the road.

'Go on, now,' he said, 'I'm eighty-two years, three months and five days. Would you believe that? I was baptized on the fourth of June, eighty-two years ago, and it's the truth I'm telling you.'

'Well, it's a great wonder,' I said, 'to think you're that age, when you're as strong as I am to this day.'

'I am not strong at all,' he went on, more despondingly, 'not strong the way I was. If I had two glasses of whiskey I'd dance a hornpipe would dazzle your eyes; but the way I am at this minute you could knock me down with a rush. I have a noise in my head, so that you wouldn't hear the river at the side of it, and I can't sleep at nights. It's that weakens me. I do be lying in the darkness thinking of all that has happened in three-score years to the families of Wicklow—what this son did, and what that son did, and of all that went across the sea, and wishing black hell would seize them that never wrote three words to say were they alive or in good health. That's the profession I have now—to be thinking of all the people, and of the times that's gone. And, begging your pardon, might I ask your name?'

I told him.

'There are two branches of the Synges in the County Wicklow,' he said, and then he went on to tell me fragments of folklore connected with my forefathers. How a lady used to ride through Roundwood 'on a curious beast' to visit an uncle of hers in Roundwood Park, and how she married one of the Synges and got her weight in gold—eight stone of gold—as her dowry: stories that referred to events which took place more than a hundred years ago.

When he had finished I told him how much I wondered at his knowledge of the country.

'There's not a family I don't know,' he said, 'from Baltinglass to the sea, and what they've done, and who they've married. You don't know me yet, but if you were a while in this place talking to myself, it's more pleasure and gratitude you'd have from my company than you'd have maybe from many a gentleman you'd meet riding or driving a car.'

By this time we had reached a wayside public-house, where he was evidently going with his can, so, as I did not wish to part with him so soon, I asked him to come in and take something with me. When we went into the little bar-room, which was beautifully clean, I asked him what he would have. He turned to the publican:

'Have you any good whiskey at the present time?' he said.

'Not now; nor at any time,' said the publican, 'we only keep bad; but isn't it all the same for the likes of you that wouldn't know the difference?'

After prolonged barging he got a glass of whiskey, took off his hat before he tasted it, to say a prayer for my future, and then sat down with it on a bench in the corner.

I was served in turn, and we began to talk about horses and racing, as there had been races in Arklow a day or two before. I alluded to some races I had seen in France, and immediately the publican's wife, a young woman who had just come in, spoke of a visit she had made to the Grand Prix a few years before.

'Then you have been in France?' I asked her.

'For eleven years,' she replied.

'Alors vous parlez Français, Madame?'

'Mais oui, Monsieur,' she answered with pure intonation.

We had a little talk in French, and then the old man got his can filled with porter—the evening drink for a party of reapers who were working on the hills—bought a pennyworth of sweets, and went back down the road.

'That's the greatest old rogue in the village,' said the publican, as soon as he was out of hearing; 'he's always making up to all who pass through the place, and trying what he can get out of them. The other day a party told me to give him a bottle of XXX porter he was after asking for. I just gave him the dregs of an old barrel we had finished, and there he was, sucking in his lips, and saying it was the finest drink ever he tasted, and that it was rising to his head already, though he'd hardly a drop of it swallowed. Faith in the end I had to laugh to hear the talk he was making.'

A little later I wished them good evening and started again on my walk, as I had two mountains to cross.

FROM THE TINKER'S WEDDING.

John Millington Synge

MARY. [*Poking out her pipe with a straw, sings.*] She'd whisper with one, and she'd whisper with two—[*She breaks off coughing.*] My singing voice is gone for this night, Sarah Casey. [*She lights her pipe.*] But if it's flighty you are itself, you're a grand, handsome woman, the glory of tinkers, the pride of Wicklow, the Beauty of Ballinacree. I wouldn't have you lying down and you lonesome to sleep this night in a dark ditch when the spring is coming in the trees; so let you sit down there by the big bough, and I'll be telling you the finest story you'd hear any place from Dundalk to Ballinacree, with great queens in it, making themselves matches from the start to the end, and they with shiny silks on them the length of the day, and white shifts for the night.

MICHAEL. [*Standing up with the tin can in his hand.*] Let you go asleep, and not have us destroyed.

MARY. [*Lying back sleepily.*] Don't mind him, Sarah Casey. Sit down now, and I'll be telling you a story would be fit to tell a woman the like of you in the springtime of the year.

SARAH. [*Taking the can from Michael, and tying it up in a piece of sacking.*] That'll not be rusting now in the dews of night. I'll put it up in the ditch the way it will be handy in the morning; and now we've that done, Michael Byrne, I'll go along with you, and welcome for Tim Flaherty's hens. [*She puts the can in the ditch.*]

MARY. [*Sleepily.*] I've a grand story of the great queens of Ireland, with white necks on them the like of Sarah Casey, and fine arms would hit you a slap the way Sarah Casey would hit you.

SARAH. [*Beckoning on the left.*] Come along now, Michael, while she's falling asleep.

[*He goes towards left. Mary sees that they are going, starts up suddenly, and turns over on her hands and knees.*]

MARY. [*Piteously.*] Where is it you're going? Let you walk back here, and not be leaving me lonesome when the night is fine.

SARAH. Don't be waking the world with your talk when we're going up through the back wood to get two of Tim Flaherty's hens are roosting in the ash-tree above at the well.

MARY. And it's leaving me lone you are? Come back here, Sarah Casey. Come back here, I'm saying; or if it's off you must go, leave me the two little coppers you have, the way I can walk up in a short while, and get another pint for my sleep.

SARAH. It's too much you have taken. Let you stretch yourself out and take a long sleep; for isn't that the best thing any woman could do, and she an old drinking heathen like yourself? [*She and Michael go out left.*]

MARY. [*Standing up slowly.*] It's gone they are and I with my feet that weak under me you'd knock me down with a rush; and my head with a noise in it the like of what you'd hear in a stream and it running between two rocks and rain falling. [*She goes over to the ditch where the can is tied in sacking, and takes it down.*] What good am I this night, God help me? What good are the grand stories I have when it's few would listen to an old woman, few but a girl maybe would be in great fear the time her hour was come, or a little child wouldn't be sleeping with the hunger on a cold night? [*She takes the can from the sacking, and fits in three empty bottles and straw in its place, and ties them up.*] Maybe the two of them have a good right to be walking out the little short while they'd be young; but if they have itself they'll not keep Mary Byrne from her full pint when the night's fine, and there's a dry moon in the sky. [*She takes up the can, and puts the package back in the ditch.*] Jemmy Neill's a decent lad; and he'll give me a good drop for the can; and maybe if I keep near the peelers to-morrow for the first bit of the fair, herself won't strike me at all; and if she does itself, what's a little stroke on your head beside sitting lonesome on a fine night, hearing the dogs barking, and the bats squeaking, and you saying over, it's a short while only till you die.

[*She goes out singing 'The Night Before Larry Was Stretched'.*]

from WAKING

Hugh Maxton

Christmas in Wicklow began very early. And once I had reached the age where I was qualified to go to communion, I opted for the earliest trip to the church about four miles north, beyond Ballinaclash. We rose in darkness, even disturbed the last of the crickets in their dark singing, and made tea quietly in the ash-warm kitchen. The concrete floor was ash-grey except where a fosset sack muffled our feet; even the shiny, even part of it had the grey intransigence of steel. Gran was asleep, with luck the children were still asleep, and a few pioneer souls prepared for the seven o'clock service. I went largely to get the business over and done with, partly to relish the chill paucity of the occasion. What gentry the congregation had attached—Captain and Mrs Kemmis, and the Hartshorns—rarely turned out at this hour. The two or three were gathered together with the impression of labour still detectable: cattle just foddered left a faint odour of hay on even the best suit, or the tiredness of last night's work mired the eye and dragged in the voice. Much of this service was, therefore, spoken and not sung: the harmonium pressed into action for just a single carol. There was electric light in the place but very early on Christmas morning its effect only cancelled the beginning of dawn in the windows; and the thin, functional, dark brown beams in the ceiling were as shadows thrown by the thin voices below. From their place among the few memorials on the walls, two rival plaques, livid Calor-gas heaters, stared down on the little congregation, adding their hiss and little concentrated heat to the ceremony. Uncle Jimmy normally went too, but because he was frequently church-warden he might return later in the morning for the second or third service. On these later occasions, his tenor warble fell from the gallery and ever failed to rouse the other voices. Betty (my mother's unmarried elder sister, who lived for a time with us in Kenilworth Park) sometimes took the early option too.

No breakfast was allowed before communion, except cups of tea to quieten the stomach rumblings. We spoke little in the kitchen, as the fire was poked into life again, a black range with blanched bars where the heat extruded, or later a tiled fire-place with a high dresser-like shelf. The turkey and ham were brought in from the dairy at the top of the yard, amid murmured comments on the price-per-pound. Jimmy took a pan loaf of white bread, and cut two slices with unusual care, murmuring perhaps a debate with himself whether a second slice was necessary. These slices were then trimmed of their crusts, a rare operation for a working tradesman whose sandwich normally was ringed with crust and oozing butter and abundant ham. These slices he trimmed, holding them steady with a heavy, calloused hand over the surface of the bread. Once trimmed, they were then cut into neat squares about half-an-inch to each side, and the little mound of bread-cubes reverently wrapped in paper. This, very shortly, would be the body of the Lord Jesus Christ for His humble Protestant followers in the parish of Ballinatone.

As we left, we debated softly the question of leaving on the yard light. This was fixed high on one corner of the house, and shone into both halves of the yard and into the entrance gate-way. The car might have been left in the bottom of the yard, away from the back-door so that the act of starting it might not waken those inside. Once out on the road, it rolled slowly down the hill under the arch of beeches, sycamores and fir-trees, unrevved for the same reverent purpose. Out from between the trees and nearing Charlie's Gate, we picked up speed and drove with still little conversation through Clash, passed the professor's house, Phelan's pub and few council cottages. At the church Jimmy went through his official preparations promptly in the vestry, and when he retired to the choir gallery (possibly the only person there) the rest of us sat in the King family pew—near the back but not so far back as to be under the choir. There was no sermon (I had noted), and the diminished ritual was thin as the wine itself, chill and unyielding as the metal taste of the chalice. 'Likewise after Supper he took the Cup...', the telescoping of an event in the remote past and its commemoration or reenactment here and now in Wicklow promised to abolish some partition in reality, yet the manifest difference between the then and the now, the Palestinian supper and the watery Irish dawn, also insisted on the falseness of futility behind notions of reenactment or convergence.

On the way back, light gathered in the sky over Jim Lawrence's. Yet westward a star was visible over our bog. Phosphorus to the learned, and debate might then rage punily as to whether we had left the yard light on, to glow yellowly through the trees. The Straight Mile lay before the car, and its mental stages were passed in reliable sequence, Ellison's gate, then the Byrnes' cottage which marked the mid-point and which housed a multitude. By the time we reached the unfinished sprawl where Willy

Leeson had opened a new entrance, the sky was ready for the full, if clouded, sun. At Carty's Corner, we turned east towards that sun, hidden though it remained by the Blue Bank. Back in the house, the general Christmas bustle had begun; the long cooking of the turkey commenced; the racket of the younger children, and the ageing faces of adults, brightened the half unveiled morning. And there was work to be done as soon as breakfast was over, the bucket and the dog contending in silvery commotion for a few last dribbles of milk.

The hours between breakfast and the next meal were ambiguous, or became so, like the yearly calendar's belittling mockery of adolescence. Were we working or not, adults or not, with duties in which pleasure should play no visible part? Should we, on the other hand, visit neighbours in some inherited sense of tradition, or simply obey our parents by going to say thank you? If we played with the things Santa gave *us*, was it to convince the even younger one of his reality?

YEATS AT GLENDALOUGH

Hugh Maxton

Still such places,
clay road leads into
placid water
ducks remark the sunlight
light drops a last spool
beyond the hedge.

Four trees before a house
imagery of a garden-seat
below the second bay
bird song off
the unaffected landscape,
stream and gliding sun.

And sweep the eye
back where you came from.
From there a stone-pine
inscribes itself
against the distance
in bold relief.

Phonepoles upright
as brushhandles
in their own composition
graph late disturbance,
bridge-piers shoulder
their coffin.

Movement intervenes
in your material,
a choked childish cry
from the master, the bloodied
bench, utterances
of the extinct motor.

See the broad lough
bask in terror
the sea's throat hope
beyond the tolerable,
between water and water
the mobile eye.

He made to live
these that seem self-born
a motion at last
to rise out of picture.
The pine-tree distances,
the house ages, its reception.

STREAM AND SUN AT GLENDALOUGH

W.B. Yeats

Through intricate motions ran
Stream and gliding sun
And all my heart seemed gay:
Some stupid thing that I had done
Made my attention stray.

Repentance keeps my heart impure;
But what am I that dare
Fancy that I can
Better conduct myself or have more
Sense than a common man?

What motion of the sun or stream
Or eyelid shot the gleam
That pierced my body through?
What made me live like these that seem
Self-born, born anew?

June 1932

FROM A FRENCHMAN'S WALK THROUGH IRELAND 1796-7

Le Chevalier de la Tocnaye

Here I paid my respects to the oldest and biggest tree to be found, not only in Ireland, but I should say in the mountains of Nice or of Provence. It is to be found in the beautiful garden of Mount Kennedy. The body of the tree is at least three feet in diameter, and wind and time having bent it to the ground, it took root in this situation, and has sent out branches of extraordinary size, so that in itself it is a little wood. Leaving here I buried myself in the passes of the arid mountains of the County of Wicklow, and came to Loughilla, one of the houses of Mr Peter Latouche. One is surprised to find such a house in such a wild and lonely place. The next house to it is at a distance of five or six miles. There are not even peasants' cabins in the neighbourhood. It is seated on a little bit of fertile earth near a beautiful lake, a bit of earth as distinct from the rest of the country as an island is from the water which surrounds it. Following the course of the stream which flows from the lake, I came to Glendalough, a word which means the valley of the two lakes. It is singular that there is not a single ancient name in this country which has not its special signification. The appropriateness here is evident, for there are really two lakes, which join at the portion of the valley called 'The Seven Churches'.

It is here in this desert that are to be found the most ancient remains of the devotion of past centuries, remains whose antiquity reaches back to the early ages of Christianity. St Kevin here founded a monastery in the third or fourth century of the Christian era, probably on the ruins of a temple of the Druids, who sought always the wildest places for the practice of their cult. This was for long a bishopric, but now it is united to that of Dublin. Here are still to be seen the ruins of seven churches, and one of those round towers of unknown origin which are so common in Ireland. They are all alike, having a door fifteen or twenty feet from the ground, generally opening eastward, some narrow windows, and inside not the slightest remains of a staircase, unless this may be found in a few projecting stones which may have served to support floors in which there must have been trap doors to allow of passing from one to another by means of ladders. These towers are always found at some distance from a church, and entirely isolated. The one which is to be seen at Brechin at Scotland is exactly of the same character.

I remember reading in the story of certain travels in the North of Asia a description of similar towers. The traveller, as far as I know, had no knowledge whatever of Ireland; he had escaped from Siberia, where, perforce, he had been living for years, and he reports having seen these extraordinary towers in that part of Tartary which lies to the north-east of the Caspian sea. He gives a little engraving of one of them, with the ruins which are near, which ruins he says are those of 'a house of prayer near which these towers are always to be found.' If it were not for the dress and faces of the thin figures appearing in the picture, one would say that the illustration was that of an Irish ruin.

Whatever these ancient buildings may have been, the Irish have now for them the greatest possible veneration. They come here from afar for pilgrimages and penitences, and on the day of the Saint, which is June 3, they dance afterwards and amuse themselves until nightfall. In this sacred enclosure are to be found remedies for many ills. Have you a pain in your arm?—it suffices to pass the limb through a hole worked in a stone, and you are free from your trouble. There is another stone on which for another ailment you shall rub your back, and another one against which you shall rub your head. And there is a pillar in the middle of the cemetery which, if you can embrace, will make you sure of your wife. The Saint's Bed is a hole about six feet long, hollowed in the rock—a very special virtue belongs to it. It is only to be reached after much trouble in scaling a steep slope of the mountain above the lake, but whoever has enough strength and resolution to climb to it, and will lie down in it, is sure never to die in childbirth. Belief in this virtue makes a great number of wives, and of girls who hope to become wives, come here to pay their devotions.

All this seemed to come in very fitly at the beginning of my travels. I pushed my arm through the hole in the stone. I rubbed my back against the rock which cures the troubles of the back, and my head against another, thus ensuring my health for the remainder of my journey. I even tried to embrace the pillar, but I cannot tell with what result. As to the Saint's Bed, I thought there was little danger of my dying from the malady against which it insures, and therefore I did not climb.

FROM THE COMPLETE WICKLOW WAY

J.B. Malone

ROUNDWOOD TO LARAGH/GLENDALOUGH
Distance: 9km
Time: 3–4 hours

A walker could hardly ask better than to be starting early from Roundwood, with bright clear weather, an easy day ahead, short in distance, lacking any great hardship.

From Roundwood go back to Lake Park crossroads, and turn left, to head SW on the tarmac road.

On the way up from Roundwood, the views east show the two Vartry ponds, as these reservoirs are locally known. The right-hand pond (1863) was the original Dublin water supply, the left-hand being the Vartry Extension (1923); both were added to in 1939, when the Poulaphouca water scheme (in West Wicklow) brought water in to the city.

The Vartry water is so pure it is claimed that even coming through Dublin taps it can be used for any purpose for which distilled water is needed—in fact, your real Dubliner will never put anything into whiskey except a small drop of Vartry water.

Discussing these and similar intriguing topics will have brought you to the descent towards Oldbridge, a bridge over the Annamoe River. The woods of Lake Park are on the right, state forest on the left, with two landmarks also on the left—the forest entrance and a former schoolhouse, now a dwelling for several years but still marked 'Sch' on some maps.

Oldbridge, just downstream of Lough Dan, is a concrete structure dating from about 1934, replacing a bridge of 1823, of which only a dated stone survives built into the eastern parapet wall of the present bridge at the northern end.

Next, at a T-junction, go left, uphill, with the pine trees and stone walling of the former Barton Estate on the left and no more than a glimpse of Lough Dan behind you. This estate belonged to a Mr Hugo in 1798. He was very active against the Irish rebels, and on his land was a tree (the 'murdering tree', long since felled) against which Hugo was alleged to have shot his victims. Sure enough, when the tree was cut down the trunk was found to be full of bullets—at just about the height of a person.

Just 2 km of tarmac road from Oldbridge brings you to the turn for a gate known as the Brusher Gate.

The Wart Stone field is on the left after you turn off right (west) from the road. It is named from a stone with a deep hollow in it, possibly a primitive handmill. The water gathered in the hollow was reputed to be a certain cure for warts. These hollowed out stones (bullauns) are especially plentiful around Glendalough, and seem to be associated with early Christian sites, hermitages perhaps, or outfarms of a large monastery. The historian Liam Price made intriguing suggestion that bullauns were introduced by Christian refugees from Roman Britain, when the pagan Saxons arrived, and the bullauns themselves were used in the making of altar bread, hence the reverence they were accorded till quite recently. After the second gate, you turn left to head south on a path on a forest firebreak, the trees here being part of fairly recent planting in Drummin townland.

The Brusher Gate, which you left behind at the end of the boreen, is traditionally the place where local people left food for the nineteenth-century rebel Michael Dwyer and his men, who held out in the recesses of these mountains for some five years after the demise of Irish resistance in Wexford following the uprising of 1798. There are wide views east on this section, over the glen of the Annamoe River to forested Castlekevin Hill, 295m, and its southerly neighbours, Moneystown, 389m, and Trooperstown (known locally as Mweeleen), 371m.

These eastern heights, being isolated from the main mountains, give memorable views on clear days. Drummin Forest firebreak ends at C, Sketches 22, 23 [*not reproduced here—ed.*], but the Way goes on south, over ferny ground, ignoring a rutted path going east down to the same road you left in favour of the Brusher Gate boreen. Now you avoid losing height, and join another firebreak path, this time above Paddock Hill Forest, leading on SSW. The next landmark is a stile in the forest fence on the right, a good place to halt and admire the western view.

The foreground is all bare moorland, scrubby heather and grazings, with scattered rocks, displaying plenty of white quartzite. Above the unseen depths of Glenmacnass valley Tonelegee Mountain (816m) rears, a wall of cliffs above hidden Lough Ouler—cliffs already seen distantly from Sleamain Mountain, but seen here from a more southerly angle, showing their giant structure of rock rib and buttress. Due west, Brockagh Mountain is revealed as an almost independent satellite of Tonelegee. The less shapely summit to NW is Moyle (called Mall Hill on some maps). Going on south, the Way drops south towards Laragh, then turns right, to cross a stile at the SE corner of forestry in Glenmacnass. From the stile a path and a forest road lead down to the Military Road. The steep path twists down through the trees, keeping fairly close to the wall of the forest, then it meets a forest road at an elbow and goes down to the gate and barrier, turning left on meeting the Military Road.

This is the highest through road, and one of the most interesting, in Ireland. We owe this road to the rebel leaders Michael Dwyer and Robert Emmet (risings of 1798 and 1803 respectively) whose rapid movements through these mountains so alarmed Dublin Castle authorities that it was speedily decided that 'something must be done!' Accordingly, around 1800, a Highland regiment was put to work here (for a shilling a day) and perhaps the grandsons of men who marched with the Jacobite Prince Charles Edward Stuart (affectionately known as the 'Bonnie Prince') in 1745 laboured here to give us this Military Road.

Presumably paperwork played its usual role in slowing the rate of construction, for Emmet was already in his grave and Dwyer transported across the seas into exile before the job was finished and the 'Redcoat' Crown solders could march in comparative ease from end to end of Wicklow, with stout barracks en route at Glencree, Laragh, Drumgoff and Aghavannagh.

About 270m further south, turn right, over a stile, to follow a mass path over the Glenmacnass Footbridge, towards Laragh Catholic church.

Once common in Ireland, mass paths, like sundry other aspects of religion, have had to face the combined assault of technology and affluence, for even the most pious parishioner will not trek two miles when he can be whisked in comfort in his own or in a neighbour's car to the church in a quarter of the time.

Mass paths are relics of an earlier time when almost every country person walked, when only the gentry and the strongest of strong farmers owned a riding horse. Walking would have been the normal way of travel, to markets, to small village shops, to cross the hill to borrow a scythe, or court a neighbour's daughter. Before Catholic Emancipation in 1829 which ended the Penal Laws by which Catholic worship was outlawed, Catholic churches were built well away from the main roads. In fact, even up to about 1870, a few extra-bigoted landlords insisted that places of Papist worship be kept outside the towns they controlled.

Similarly schoolpaths from farms to the schoolhouse also fell into disuse when school buses started to collect the pupils.

By this attractive mass path you come over the Chapel Lane, turning left for Laragh from the stile.

At the gate of St Kevin's Church, fork right if making for accommodation at Glendalough An Óige hostel; otherwise fork left for a selection of other accommodation in Laragh.

If you have started reasonably early from Roundwood, you will have a half day left to explore historic Glendalough, the round tower, the seven churches (not forgetting St Saviour's, the most highly decorated of all), the twin lakes, and perhaps even the isolated Van Dieman's mines, high above the Upper Lough.

ST KEVIN AND THE BLACKBIRD

Seamus Heaney

And then there was St Kevin and the blackbird.
The saint is kneeling, arms stretched out, inside
His cell, but the cell is narrow, so

One turned-up palm is out the window, stiff
As a crossbeam, when a blackbird lands
And lays in it and settles down to nest.

Kevin feels the warm eggs, the small breasts, the tucked
Neat head and claws and, finding himself linked
Into the network of eternal life,

Is moved to pity: now he must hold his hand
Like a branch out in the sun and rain for weeks
Until the young are hatched and fledged and flown.

And since the whole thing's imagined anyhow,
Imagine being Kevin. Which is he?
Self-forgetful or in agony all the time

From the neck on out down through his hurting forearms?
Are his fingers sleeping? Does he still feel his knees?
Or has the shut-eyed blank of underearth

Crept up through him? Is there distance in his head?
Alone and mirrored clear in love's deep river,
'To labour and not to seek reward', he prays,

A prayer his body makes entirely
For he has forgotten self, forgotten bird
And on the riverbank forgotten the river's name.

A LETTER TO MARIA EDGEWORTH

Sir Walter Scott

Steven's Green, 27th July 1825

My dear friend,—I am just returned from Wicklow delighted with all I have seen. The mere wood water and wilderness have not so much the charm of novelty for a North as for a South Briton. But these are intermingled with an appearance of fertility which never accompanies them in our land and with a brilliancy of verdure which justifies your favourite epithet of the green Isle. The ruins at the Seven Churches are singularly curious—the oldest places where the Christian faith was taught and which still remain standing. I fear they will not stand long unless measures are taken to preserve them. I was seized with a return of a spirit of enterprise once the most familiar of my attributes, and scrambled up into St Kevin's bed. My Kathleen on the occasion was an old soldier's wife of the bloody Connaughts as she called them. She was much offended at some one who told her afterwards that I was a poet—for she was sure she said I was no poet but a noble generous gentleman for I had given her half a crown.

FROM GLENDALLOCH

William Drennan

Th'enchantment of the place has bound
All Nature in a sleep profound;
And silence of the ev'ning hour
Hangs o'er Glendalloch's hallow'd tow'r;
A mighty grave-stone, set by Time,
That, 'midst these ruins, stands sublime,
To point the else-forgotten heaps,
Where princes and where prelates sleep;
Where Tuathal rests th'unnoted head,
And Keivin finds a softer bed:
'Sods of the soil' that verdant springs
Within the sepulchre of kings.

Here—in the circling mountain's shade,
In this vast vault, by Nature made,
Whose tow'ring roof excludes the skies
With savage Kyle's stupendous size;
With Lugduff heaves his moory height,
And giant Broccagh bars the light;
Here—when the British spirit, broke,
Had fled from Nero's iron yoke,
And sought this dreary dark abode,
To save their altars and their God,
From cavern black, with mystic gloom,
(Cradle of Science, and its tomb,)
Where Magic had its early birth,
Which drew the Sun and Moon to earth,
From hollow'd rock, and devious cell,
Where Mystery was fond to dwell,
And, in the dark and deep profound,
To keep th'eternal secret bound,
(Recorded by no written art,
The deep memorial of the heart,)

In flowing robe, of spotless white,
Th'Arch-Druid issued forth to light;
Brow-bound with leaf of holy oak,
That never felt the woodman's stroke.
Behind his head a crescent shone,
Like to the new-discover'd moon;
While, flaming, from his snowy vest,
The plate of judgment clasp'd his breast.
Around him press'd the illumin'd throng,
Above him rose the light of song;
And from the rocks and woods around
Return'd the fleet-wing'd sons of sound.

'Maker of Time! we mortals wait
To hail thee at thy Eastern gate;
Where, these huge mountains thrown aside,
Expands for thee a portal wide.
Descend upon this altar, plac'd
Amidst Glendalloch's awful waste:
So shall the paean of thy praise
Arise, to meet thy rising rays,
From Elephanta's sculptur'd cave,
To Eire, of the Western wave;
And the rejoicing earth prolong
The orbit of successive song:
For we by thy reflection shine—
Who knows our God, becomes divine.'

THE PRIORY OF ST SAVIOUR, GLENDALOUGH

Donald Davie

A carving on the jamb of an embrasure,
'Two birds affronted with a human head
Between their beaks' is said to be
'Uncertain in its significance but
A widely known design.' I'm not surprised.

For the guidebook cheats: the green road it advises
In fact misled; and a ring of trees
Screened in the end the level knoll on which
St Saviour's, like a ruin on a raft,
Surged through the silence.

I burst through brambles, apprehensively
Crossed an enormous meadow. I was there.
Could holy ground be such a foreign place?
I climbed the wall, and shivered. There flew out
Two birds affronted by my human face.

FROM OMEROS

Derek Walcott

Though all its wiry hedgerows startle the spirit,
when the ancient letters rise to a tinker's spoon,
banging a saucepan, those fields which they inherit

hide stones white-knuckled with hatred. A pitted moon
mounted the green pulpit of Sugar Loaf Mountain
in its wax-collar. Along a yew-guarded road,

a cloud hung from a branch in the orange hour,
like a shirt that was stained with poetry and with blood.
The wick of the cypress charred. Glen-da-Lough's tower.

GLENDALOUGH'S ROUND TOWER

Dave Smith

Phallic, its speckled gray stone seems to leap up
in time mild as the valley road that uncoils
where the car park yawns with crowds. Dennis and I
dawdle, our wives snap photos of vaults as light
fails ahead. We stumble upon them, their lens set,
the Irish family on holiday: red-topped father,
now buzz-cut and ear-ringed, half punk, half Viking.
She's whipped, pale as ground flour, infant like a fruit
hung from her breast, five more shifting, hands clasped,
climbing to the slabbed stairstep. They grunt at stones
that pave the ground where western sun slices eyes
used to squinting. They want to play, the oldest
girl's frock lifting at gusts or the lad's first poke.

FOR DENNIS O'DRISCOLL

WINTER IN GLENMACNASS

Harry Clifton

Valley opening south, when I was lost
To everyone but myself, I looked around me
At condensations of mist
Into waterdrops, into cold infinities
Crystallising like laws
On the dripping haws

Of a back road through the mountains.
Crushed, they would ooze
Unreadiness, bitter and yellow,
The colour of fields gone fallow
And drained of intention, all patience
Like myself, for the news

That was about to begin.
If I had a future
Inside me, it would have to wait
Where instinct buried it, under my hesitations.
Instead, this recess of nature,
This state of grace before sin

Was closing me in
Like Eden, from cities and years
Before me and behind… I'd abandoned my car
Back there in the world of men,
To watch the lines of power
Sag northward, disappear

Among snowlines, windy gaps
And acts of God. Already, I was gone
If I only knew it, there where forests of pine
Were inland seas, for the mind to set sail on—
Steady whisperings, rooted and free
Like desire, like memory.

KILLALANE

Thomas Kinsella

I
I have known the hissing assemblies.
The preference for the ease of the spurious
—the measured poses and stupidities.

On a fragrant slope descending into the fog
over our foul ascending city
I turned away in refusal,
and held a handful of high grass
sweet and grey to my face.

II
We sat face to face at the kitchen table
silent in the morning cold,
our bodies and minds clean.

Outside a faint coarse call
came from a throat high in the light
and, higher up the valley,
a coarse quiet throat-answer

—our raven couple talking together,
flying up toward their place
on the high rock shoulder.

III
A pair of light deer
sailing back and forth
up the hill through the high grass
on their accurate feet

stopped to look back at their mess
scattered around our back door,
then disappeared
in among the trees.

IV
I left the road where a stile entered the wood,
the dry trees standing quiet in their own dust,
bare branches with sharp fingers out everywhere.

Faced suddenly with a mouse body
upside down, staring, on a patch of bark.
The shape small, the wings flat

meant only to be half seen
quick in the half light: little leather angel
falling everywhere, snapping at the invisible.

FROM MEDIEVAL WICKLOW–'A LAND OF WAR'

J.F. Lydon

Medieval Wicklow was a war-torn and dangerous place. The invasion of the Scots under Edward Bruce in 1315 provoked a rising against the king by the Wicklow Irish, involving wholesale massacres and church-burnings. Among the most unusual phenomena thrown up by this period is the Wicklow heretic Adam Duff O'Toole, described here by J.F. Lydon in an extract from his essay 'Medieval Wicklow—"A Land of War"'. The Hoggen Green referred to is the site of the present-day Trinity College, Dublin.

Adam Duff O'Toole was convicted of heresy in 1327. He denied the Incarnation of Christ, said that there could not possibly be three persons in one God, asserted that the Blessed Mary, mother of the Lord, was a prostitute, denied the resurrection of the dead, insisted that the sacred scriptures were nothing more than a collection of fables, and denounced as false the Holy See. On 11 April 1328 Adam was burned as a heretic on Hoggen Green in Dublin. Some years later, when the Irish government was responding to the famous remonstrance addressed by O'Neill to Pope John XXII, O'Toole's heresy was produced as evidence of the depravity of the Irish. It was said that because of his 'perverse doctrine... many souls among the Irish were lost and damned.'

FROM THE ANNALS OF THE FOUR MASTERS

'The Four Masters'

The Annals of the Kingdom of Ireland, *also known as the* Annals of the Four Masters, *were written between 1632 and 1636 by Micheál Ó Cléirigh, Cúchoigríche Ó Cléirigh, Fearfeasa Ó Maoilchonaire and Cúchoigríche Ó Duibhgeannáin and other scribes in the Franciscan friary at Bundrowse, County Donegal. This extract describes the flight to Wicklow of Hugh O'Donnell and Henry and Art O'Neill in 1591. Art's Cross, a memorial to Art O'Neill, can still be found in Glenree high in the Wicklow Gap. The translation quoted here is John O'Donovan's (1848–1851).*

Hugh Roe, the son of Hugh, son of Manus O'Donnell, remained in Dublin, in prison and in chains, after his first escape, to the winter of this year. One evening he and his companions, Henry and Art, the sons of O'Neill (John), before they had been brought into the refection house, took an advantage of the keepers, and knocked off their fetters. They afterwards went to the privy-house, having with them a very long rope, by the loops of which they let themselves down through the privy-house, until they reached the deep trench that was around the castle. They climbed the outer side, until they were on the margin of the trench. A certain faithful youth, who was in the habit of visiting them, and to whom they had communicated their secret, came to them at this time, and guided them. They then proceeded through the streets of the city, mixing with the people; and no one took more notice of them than of any one else, for they did not delay at that time to become acquainted with the people of the town; and the gates of the city were wide open. They afterwards proceeded by every intricate and difficult place, until they arrived upon the surface of the Red Mountain over which Hugh had passed in his former escape. The darkness of the night, and the hurry of their flight (from dread of pursuit), separated the eldest of them from the rest, namely, Henry O'Neill. Hugh was the greenest of them with respect to years, but not with respect to prowess. They were grieved at the separation of Henry from them; but, however, they proceeded onwards, their servant guiding them along. That night was snowing, so that it was not easy for them to walk, for they were without [sufficient] clothes or coverings, having left their outer garments behind them in the privy-house, through which they had escaped. Art was more exhausted by this rapid journey than Hugh, for he had been a long time in captivity, and had become very corpulent from long confinement in the prison. It was not so with Hugh; he had not yet passed the age of boyhood, and had not [yet] done growing and increasing at this period, and his pace and motion were quick and rapid. When he perceived Art had become feeble, and that his step was becoming inactive and slow, he requested him to place one arm upon his own shoulder, and the other upon that of the servant. In this manner they proceeded on their way, until they had crossed the Red Mountain, after which they were weary and fatigued, and unable to help Art on any further; and as they were not able to take him with them, they stopped to rest under the shelter of a high rocky precipice which lay before them. On halting here, they sent the servant to bring the news to Glenmalure, where dwelt Fiagh, the son of Hugh [O'Byrne], who was then at war with the English. This is a secure and impregnable valley; and many prisoners who escaped from Dublin were wont to resort to that valley, for they considered themselves secure there, until they could return to their own country. When the servant came into the presence of Fiagh, he delivered his message, and how he had left the youths who had escaped from the city, and [stated] that they would not be overtaken alive unless he sent them relief instantly. Fiagh immediately ordered some of his servants of truth (those in whom he had most confidence) to go to them, taking with them a man to carry food, and another to carry ale and beer. This was accordingly done, and they arrived at the place where the men were. Alas! unhappy and miserable was their condition on their arrival. Their bodies were covered over with white-bordered shrouds of hail-stones freezing around them on every side, and their light clothes and fine-threaded shirts too adhered to their skin; and their large shoes and leather thongs to their shins and feet; so that, covered as they were with the snow, it did not appear to the men who had arrived that they were human beings at all, for they found no life in their members, but just as if they were dead. They were raised by them from their bed, and they requested of them to take some of the meat and drink; but they were not able to avail themselves of it, for every drink they took they rejected again on the instant; so that Art at length died, and was buried in that place. As to Hugh, after some time, he retained the beer; and, after drinking it, his energies were restored, except the use of his two feet, for they were dead members, without feeling, swollen and blistered by the frost and snow. The men carried him to the valley which we have mentioned, and he was placed in a sequestered house, in a solitary part of a dense wood, where he remained under cure until a messenger came privately from his brother-in-law, the Earl O'Neill, to inquire after him. When the messenger arrived, he [Hugh] prepared to depart. It was difficult for him to undertake that journey, for his feet could not have been healed [within the time], so that another person had to raise him on his horse, and to lift him from his horse, whenever he wished to alight. Fiagh dispatched a troop of horse with him, [who accompanied him] until he crossed the River Liffey, to protect him against the snares which were laid for him; for the English of Dublin had heard that Hugh was at Glenmalure, and had therefore posted guards on the shallow fords of the river, to prevent him and the prisoners who had escaped along with him from passing into Ulster. The youths who were along with Hugh were obliged to cross a difficult deep ford on the River Liffey, near the city of Dublin; and they proceeded on their way until they came to the green of the fortress, unperceived by the English. The people by whom he had been abandoned some time before, after his first escape, namely, Felim O'Toole and his brother, were amongst the troop who escorted him to this place; and they made friendship and amity with each other. They bade him farewell, and having given him their blessing, departed from him.

FROM THE BOOK OF THE O'BYRNES

The Leabhar Branach, *or* Book of the O'Byrnes, *is the poem-book of four generations of the ruling family of the O'Byrnes of Gabhal Raghnuill in West Wicklow, and dates from c. 1550–1630. Two poems from the book are reproduced here, one in translation and one in the original Irish. The first, by Aonghus Mac Doighri Í Dhálaigh, is dedicated to the clan's most famous member, the fierce and bellicose Fiach MacHugh; Edward Lawson's translation appeared in the second volume of James Hardiman's* Irish Minstrelsy *(1841). The second poem, written by Donnchadh Ó Fíláin in the séadna metre, describes the residence of the O'Byrne chiefs at Ballincor in Glenmalure.*

ODE TO THE MILESIANS

God shield you, champions of the Gaël,
Never may your foes prevail;
Never were ye known to yield,
Basely in the embattled field.

Generous youths, in glittering arms,
Rouse at glory's shrill alarms;
Fight for your green native hills,
And flowery banks of flowing rills.

Ireland, to avenge or save,
Many a conflict you must brave;
And on rough crags in storms and snows,
Snatch a short though sound repose.

Slow to wrest your father's land
From the foreign spoiler's hand;
You forget its fields of flowers,
Its stately palaces and towers.

Not for lack of heart or nerve,
Bloated foreigners we serve;
Would to heaven, united all,
We resolved to stand or fall.

Oh grief of heart! proscribed at home,
Dispersed, our chiefs and princes roam
Through gloomy glens and forests wild,
Hunted like wolves—banditti stiled.

While a rude remorseless horde,
O'er our lovely vallies lord;
Their vengeful hosts, who round us close,
Rob my long nights of sweet repose.

Nor till you prostrate them in gore,
Can rapture thrill my bosom's core;
Empurpled squadrons bright in arms,
Your perils rack me with alarms.

No less will glut their savage hate,
Than root and branch to extirpate:
God guide and guard you day and night,
And chiefly in the dreadful fight.

Forth warriors, forth, with heaven to speed,
Proud in your country's cause to bleed;
They best may hope the victor's wreath,
Whose watch word's 'liberty or death'.

Beannacht ag Baile na Corra

Beannacht ag Baile na Corra,
  mo chuairt ann is aithghearr liom;
ní fhuil no thol dún ag díorghadh
  [is] dol ón dún fhíonmhar fhionn.

Baile na Corra ar gcuan sealga,
  seanróimh oinigh Innsi Néill,
beag an t-iongnadh buadh 'gá bhuidhnibh
  d'iolradh na sluagh suilbhir séimh.

Mo bheannacht féin fágbhuim agaibh,
  a fhuil Raghnaill na reacht suairc;
bhar meadh ga héineang a n-uighinn
  feadh Éireann dá gcuirinn cuairt?

MARCHING SONG OF FEAGH MACHUGH O'BYRNE
A.D. 1580

Patrick Joseph McCall

(It is a tradition that this air ('Follow me up to Carlow') was first performed by the pipers of Feagh MacHugh as he marched to attack Carlow after his victory over Lord Deputy Grey at Glenmalure. MacCahir Ogue was Brian MacCahir Cavanagh, whom Fitzwilliam had driven out of his possessions.)

Lift, MacCahir Ogue, your face,
Brooding o'er the old disgrace,
That black Fitzwilliam stormed your place,
    And drove you to the Fern!
Grey said victory was sure—
Soon the firebrand he'd secure;
Until he met at Glenmalure,
    Feagh MacHugh O'Byrne!

Chaunt:
Curse and swear, Lord Kildare!
Feagh will do what Feagh will dare—
Now, Fitzwilliam have a care!
    Fallen is your star, low!
Up with halbert, out with sword!
On we go; for, by the Lord!
Feagh MacHugh has given the word—
    Follow me up to Carlow!

See the swords at Glen Imayle
Flashing o'er the English Pale!
See all the children of the Gael
    Beneath O'Byrne's banners!
Rooster of a fighting stock,
Would you let a Saxon cock
Crow out upon an Irish rock?
    Fly up, and teach him manners!

Chaunt:
Curse and swear, Lord Kildare! etc

From Tasaggart to Clonmore,
Flows a stream of Saxon gore!
Och, great is Rory Ogue O'More
      At sending loons to Hades!
White is sick, and Lane is fled!
Now for black Fitzwilliam's head—
We'll send it over dripping red
To Liza and her ladies!

Chaunt:
Curse and swear, Lord Kildare! etc

FROM THE LIFE AND ADVENTURES OF JOSEPH HOLT

Joseph Holt

We traveled on towards Dublin. This young man was from Castlepollard, with three cars loaded with eggs. Their name was Kenedy. There were four in company with me, three of which were 'United.' Gentle reader, I think it my duty to let you know as great a number of military forces as could be spared from duty were in pursuit of my fellow sufferers.

I made it up with the owners of sd cars that I should personate the owner, and every party of army I met seemed quite busy doing some security to my loading, and when I perceived any army drinking at a door, I stopped and called for drink, wishing them every success in their pursuit, and in all the men I met that day, not one seemed to know me—but one, who smiled a knowledge of me.

I arived save [safe] to Park End Street, where Kenedys and I went into an alehouse, drank half a pint of punch. So we parted. They wished me safe through Dublin.

I directed my way over Old [B?]ow bridge and passed by Old Kilmainham, through James's St, Thos [Thomas] Street and Francis St, turned at the Cross Poddle through New St, through Harold's Cross, but was known by a weoman, name of Susy Needam [Needham], who was reared at Delginny [Delgany] in the County of Wicklow, who sent word to Mr Berresford [Beresford], who sent his corps after me. I heard the sound of their horses' feet coming up. I instantly scaled the wall. I lay down close by its side.

A little above me, they met a man whom the[y] asked did he meet a person giving my description? He answered, 'No.'

Says they, 'He is gone towards Crumlin.'

As soon as the[y] advanced at a convenient distance, I rescaled the wall and crossed the wall opposite.

I then took the field up to Holly Park, crossing over by Lady de [C?]ily's and up to Mount Pelia [Montpelier]—that enchanted house. Gentle Reader, I passed by the house that day where my dr wife an children were. Had I called to see them, I should never see them more, but I hope the Almighty shie[?]d[ed?] me to die a happy death. When I arived at sd enchanted house I was much fatigued. I considered that I was arived once more in a country which I knew. I composed my[s]elf that the name of Inchantment was not able to deter me. I contemplated, 'There is nothing worse than I am,' and, in God's name, I said my prayers and slept soundly.

Next morning I aroes [*sic*], came from my arched room. I viewed it, an then advanced to Pipers town, a small village, where I found a piper who played 'Erin go bragh' at end of the former late Rebellion. I saw a small girl, whom I asked did she know Holts of Bonabreena [Bohernabreena], or the Chaper [Chapel] House. I instantly wrote to my brother, requesting of him to send me a loaf of bread, some cheese and a pint of whiskey. On receiving the note he said to his wife, 'Joseph is not dead, as here is his hand writing.' He sent the contents of my note and a note with it to meet him near Carys Field.

On coming to sd field I found him in company with a Richard Johnson, a farmer who lived in Kipper [Kippure]. We sat together and talked of part of my adventures. Johnson proposed to go to Mr Beresford to obtain my pardon. I was afraid of him, which I had reason to be, as hereafter will appear, as in my later absence he took a cow from my distressed wife and never paid her. His ungratefullness was dowbly criminal, for he had 5 horses taken by men to Whelp Rock, which I caused to be restored to him, which convinced me that his proffered kindness was but to deceive, together with the large sum was offered to whom should have me taken.

I now once more had the gratification of seeing my much afflicted wife. At this time my hopes despaired much of obtaining an escape. I said to my wife, should I hear of His Majestie's Pardon, I should then resign. So I bid her farewell and commenced recruiting on[c]e more.

On leaving Glenasmole I crossed Butter Mountain, going Ballyfolen [Ballyfolan] Pass to Scorleck's Lep [Scurlock's Leap], halted in Adown [Athdown]. I went to a widow Kirwan's house, asked hur for some refreshment. She declared she was destitute of any thing save some cabage leaves which were in the pot. I drew my sword and with it examined sd pot, found that part of her confession was right, but knew she told me a lye for, in a few days after, I directed some of the men, with liberty to strictly examine her house, where they discovered two pieces of bacon, four sacks of oat male.

Notwithstanding her ungratefulness to me, some time prior to it I had hur cleared of ten pound fine for depredations she committed on a plantation of Peter Latouche [La Touche], Esqr. at Lugalaw. Her explanation

I insert to let the reader know her ingratitude and how I treated her at my return. I proceeded to Ballydonnell, to a Simeon Kerney's [Simon Kearney's], where I was received with the warmest kindness, the[n] was instantly furnished with plenty of good refreshment. They entreated me to stop all night, but I refused. I bed them farewell, going to Ballylow, from thence to Whelp Rock.

They received me with acclamations of joy. They wished Ide stop there but did not think it prudent, as I was informed many wounded creatures was in Glenmaller [Glenmalure] and knew they were much in want of one to dress their sores. I then passed over the Three Lough Mountain. Crossing it, I came up to a young woman whom I knew. She collected for me some froughins [froughans], a small black fruit whech grows on elevated places. We bot[h] sat down, and pass[ed] part of sd evening pleasant, as we were in such a retired place. I saved this young weoman's life in Longwood by rescuing her from the army. I received two small wounds. One of her brothers was killed at Clonard, and another wounded at Castlecarbury.

Sd young woman advanced with me to Glenmuller. We stopped at the house of Pierce Harny [Harney]. Sd Glen is about 21 miles in length, its breadth is uniqual—the widest not more than 3/4 of a mile. The mountains forming sd Glen is remarkably high and many parts inaccessible, treatning to crush the beholders by their fall.

THE DESTRUCTION OF POETIC HABITAT

Biddy Jenkinson

In a glen in County Wicklow, a fold in the hills between the great valleys of Glendalough and Glenmalure, there is a spring well, the source of the Derrybawn brook. Once upon a time I felt that this was my own personal 'Sidhe of Nechtáin'.

I understood that if I approached it at the proper time, under the proper circumstances, and in a state of grace, a gush of water would spurt from it and blind me with inspiration, as Bóinn was blinded at Nechtáin's Well, and that a wave of poetry would rise to pursue me, as Bóinn was pursued, so that I should leave a wake of poems after me forever more as Bóinn trails the river Boyne.

Poetic inspiration, unless of course it is committed to rising elsewhere, should rise in a holy well where it will be whisked by the tail fins of brown trout, who keep the gravel untarnished, who face always into the pulse of the water, and who eat only rowan-berries.

My well was halfway up Sleefionn, surrounded by larch trees in a green declivity cropped tight by rabbits. Here the Derrybawn brook ran gently from the crotch of the hill. It was a serene place, gentle to the senses after a struggle through heather, bracken, and the Irish gorse that does not grow erect and avoidable like the Scottish variety but yips and nicks the ankles like an agitated Imaal terrier.

To lie in an attitude under the swishing branches listening to the sob of the water must surely be the proper thing for an aspiring writer of poetry. It was there that I composed my very first poem. Oddly enough I wrote it in English, English being the language of ceremony, of gravestones, of official purposes. My first poem was an official one, an elegy for a tom-cat with a crooked paw. I had nursed him through an accident with a rabbit trap only to see him flattened by the very first tour bus that took the bend in the newly-metalled road to Glenmalure.

That tour bus was a definitive benchmark for the advance of civilisation in the valley, and I am glad that I began to write at such a clearly defined point. The poem itself must have been a marvel. All I can remember of it is the last two lines: 'Poor crook leg Tom / has gone to hunt amid the stars.'

The well is no longer holy. Progress, heralded by the bus tour, advanced through the valley on the wheels of EEC subsidies. The brook is a brown, algae-clogged rivulet where no trout stir. The heather and furze have, in many places, surrendered to the carpet-bagging bracken, host to clouds of flies and midges that rise like demon angels to blacken the sky on calm days. Ground once open to all those who lived in the valley for grazing, turf cutting, tadpole hunting, has been enclosed. The population had dwindled and there was little resistance. Nobody fought to maintain rights of way. Deer farming gave way to intensive sheep farming. Now the sheep have gone down the brook in the wake of the trout. Grants and subsidies favour forestry.

The holdings in the valley had the use of three ordinary, everyday wells located in a line close to the valley floor. One of them was in Tim's Bog. It had brown water in it. Corrobetes lived in the gravel bottom, building shiny mica tunnels around their soft selves. It was the proper well for a young naturalist-poet, and its smooth surface would reflect long, dipping hair (but blur pimples), while passing clouds would conjure shadowy lovers among the water spiders. All around the bog cotton waved, gleaming white in sunlight. Fancy wove bright shrouds of it. Melancholy is exquisitely stimulating to the poetic sensibilities of the young. Tim's Bog has now been drained and planted.

Enormous sheds have been erected close to Nailie's Well. For a while the users of the well convinced themselves that the effluvia of the deer and, later, of the sheep concentrated in these sheds was quite innocuous. Then they stopped drinking it unless it was boiled and stewed with tea. Then they made other arrangements. The well filled in. The land was drained. Nailie MacGúgáin used to live there under enormous beech trees long ago. According to local speculation—and I am not one to set a limit to the advance of imagination in the territory of history—the name Nailie came to the area with the O'Neills. The O'Neills came here in the sixteenth century to help Fiach Mac Hugh O'Byrne of Glenmalure in his stand against the forces of Queen Elizabeth.

The young, patriotic poet used to make atonement at this well. Her ancestors had been Sassenachs, much to her disgust. Her reflection in Nailie's Well assured her frequently that had she lived in those times, her deeds of derring-do would have made a difference to the course of history. Fiach Mac Hugh would never have been slain; his quartered limbs would never have been exposed on hurdles outside Dublin Castle. His head would never have been pickled and sent to Queen Elizabeth. I pity any young poet who has no place in which to reflect her flashing brow and anachronistic chivalry.

The third well was fenced off from us for a while. The water, however, is too pure, the place itself too beautiful to be surrendered. Buckets are still carried up and down the steep narrow path where Granny, coming up with two brimming zinc buckets met Grandfather (on his way down with empty buckets) and accepted his proposal of marriage without spilling a drop. This is the most romantic of wells, a place for an adolescent poet to linger by moonlight, dreaming of demon lovers. A mossy cliff, a grotto, and a fountain of the clearest, bluest, coldest water on earth. It is called Foley's Well, and it lies on the Derrybawn side of the brook.

Foley, according to oral tradition, had a little sweetshop at the bend of the Cullentra road at the start of one of the great zigzags built by the British in the eighteenth century to allow their ox-drawn caravans access to the hills in order to crush insurgency. The outline of the military road is still visible. Occasionally, by moonlight, the redcoats stop at the stones that mark Foley's shop to purchase bull's-eyes and hard-boiled sweets and wash them down with draughts of well water before tackling the long haul to Drumgoff barracks. It is possible to hear them in those quiet moments when the senses are alert and the busy brain is still—providing, of course, that one has not sinned against the abiding spirit of the place.

There were other springs in the valley that I would like to commemorate. One of them is in the spruce wood planted by the *Roinn Foraoise* after Independence. There was a dwelling named 'Hunters' high on the hill. Nobody remembers who the Hunters were. All they left was a pile of stones, a few lonesome trees, and the well. This well had no bottom. It was wide and black and fleshy at the mouth with roiling walls of moss... so my mother remembers it. She saw it once as a child and she has remembered it on behalf of the next two generations. For safety Hunters' Well was boarded up with planks when the forest was planted... 'But they are all rotten by now,' said my mother. 'They are just waiting for the unwary foot. For heaven's sake be careful!'

Not knowing the precise location of 'Hunters', all my childhood walks in the wood were rendered exhilarating by the possibility that the earth at any moment might open under my feet and swallow me up. Every poet needs to walk occasionally in fear of the sky falling or the earth moving, in full awareness of the uncertainty of things and the joy of living, if only for a minute.

My father, in his late seventies, decided to 'bring in the water' for me. He ran a pipe to the hill well. It was outside the property line, but used by at least four generations of Jenkinsons. He was enormously proud of his labour, the last task of its kind he was able to undertake. The pipe ended in a modern tap fixed to a stake in a field. There was a ceremonious turning-on ceremony. The water bubbled out. It was pronounced better even than Foley's Well. I paid tribute to it in my second book of poetry, *Uiscí Beatha*, with a photo of the tap and stake. By some serendipitous error the printer turned the photo upside down, and in some of the books my tap pours upwards… not at all a bad thing in a book entitled *Waters of Life*.

That well was ploughed up by our local entrepreneur, and the water joined the rest of the run-off from the hill in a roaring gully down past his sheep sheds to the brook. My tap and stake still stand, and the pipe dangles over the ditch. Last Sunday the piper, Seosamh Ó Dubhghaill, came to the old house and played a lament for the ghosts, and jigs and reels to set them dancing. He composed a march extempore, on the spot that I have been allowed to name 'Tobar an Tí' (The Well of the House). And so, in a sense, the flow continues.

There is a quagmire west of Derrybawn Mountain, towards Lugduff, a different kind of well. There, under a quaking emerald skin, under gallons of ale-coloured bogwater, lie the bones of Cainneach. Cainneach was the wife of Colmán, a king of Leinster who converted to Christianity in the time of St Kevin and sent their son Faelán to Glendalough for his third-level education. Cainneach, wise woman and decent pagan that she was, climbed Bóthar na gCró and went to a place where she could look down into Glendalough. When she saw St Kevin lead his followers in procession through the valley, she hurled a curse down at him. The saint, the Christian God being in the ascendant, had greater power than she and turned the curse back on her. The hill softened under her feet and swallowed her. The place is known as *Láithreach Chainneach*; in English, 'the Hag's Slough'.

Cainneach is still there. Under the sheep dung and the barbed wire and the rampant bracken there is a presence. Something survives that is not of our *gaimbín* present. What this thing may be, how to find it, whether to name it or not, and how to revere it: issues for the older writer plodding through the heather in August, gilt with heather dust and humbled out of all pretensions by the silence of the hills.

CUAIRT AN CHLÁRAITHEORA AR GHLEANN DÁ LOCH

Biddy Jenkinson

Tá uisce an leá faoi mo bhuataisí.
Bíonn treá ar leith san uisce seo a shníonn
ina fhuil gheimhridh ó chruacha sneachta na gclaíocha,
ó dhroimeanna coscartha na síne…

Níor bhorr an saol go fóill.
Tá fionnachruth ar fhéar an gharraí dhuibh
is loime cré sa bhuaile.
Tá blás fionnchorcra fuachta ar na beitheanna
ar bhóthar Chaoimhín faoi gheataí a dhísirt.
Mar seo a thagadh an Cláraitheoir.

Ní fheiceadh manaigh Ghleann Dá Loch an Cláraitheor chucu.
Thagadh sé faoi scáil Cham a' Dhoire, thar Loch na hOnchon
trí Ghleann na Samhadh
le fána
de thruslóga móra,
i gcomhléim
le heitleogaí an tsrutha lena ais
thar thulacha seansneachta
'Leabhar an Bháis' ina ucht,
mairbh Thamlachta sínte taobh le taobh
ar leathanach úr na bliana;
fómhar dhoineann an Dá Loch le cur leo,
tráthnóna idir Geimhreadh agus Earrach.

Ghlacadh sé cóngar na fáschoille
i gcumar an dá ghleann
agus thagadh sé anoir aduaidh ar na manaigh
i gcónaí.
Bhuailtí creill na marbh ar a theacht.
D'inscrítí.
Chuirtí líne idir bás is beatha.

Táimse ag fionraí ar an gCláraitheoir
im bhróga báite, in íochtar Ghleann na Samhadh
idir dhá sholas.
Tá liúr na néal ag rith chugam síos le fána
is dreoilín easpaig ar eiteall le mí-fhoighid
sa roschoill taobh liom.

I gcomhsholas fear is tor
léimeann an sruth go postúil thar na clocha
is manach dubh ag seasamh leis sa rás,
a thaca ar an ngaoith, a chlóca dubh
ag déanamh sciatháin.

Is cuirim clabhsúr ar an nGeimhreadh dubhach
le lúcháir seanmhanaigh
a scinn go buach cathréimeach
—is gan coinne ar bith—
ón gClárathcoir
thar líne
bliain dá raibh
go bhfaca sé fiondruiniú an dá loch liath,
sailchuacha, samhaircíní is fionnscoth bláth
ag fás aníos ar lorg an mhanaigh dhuibh
ón nGleann amach
soir ag an Abhainn Mhór.

CROPPY BIDDY DOLAN
FROM THE POSTHUMOUS PAPERS OF LUKE CULLEN

Luke Cullen

This woman, who acquired much notoriety during the insurrection of 1798, and for some time after that period, was born in Carnew, in the County Wicklow, about the year 1779, and was in her nineteenth year when the rebellion broke out. Her father followed the humble profession of a thatcher, and was generally from home. Her mother paid no attention whatever to the education or morals of her daughter. Let me at once apologize for being obliged to allude to immorality. But in history we can leave nothing to the imagination—truth, however repugnant, must be honestly told. And in this case, that posterity may know even the vilest of the many instruments that were used to aid the blightful Legislative Union of our country.

At ten or eleven years of age this wayward and abandoned girl was sure to be found among rude little boys at their sports, particularly riding the asses of tinkers, when any of them would sojourn in the outlets of Carnew or at a neighbouring forge, where horses were usually brought to be shod; and if she could get up on one of them, or procure any person to lift her up, she was sure to sit astride and gallop the animal up and down the street. She had an extraordinary passion for horse-riding, and at sixteen years of age could manage the quadruped at his full speed. And in the year 1798 she mostly rode with the rebel cavalry—a buxom *vivandiere* on horseback. Her lack of morals and indecencies are too disgusting to follow, but it will be sufficient to say, that this pampered informer of the county Wicklow, at thirteen years of age, was an avowed and proclaimed harlot, steeped in every crime that her age would permit of; and her precocity in vice, as it was to maturity, was singular. On her own oath, she attended night meetings at seventeen years of age, where a great number of United Irishmen assembled, about two miles from the residence of her father. After the rebellion broke out, she joined the rebel army, and soon obtained a horse, and was foremost in all the deeds of iniquity during the time the people held out in arms. But her intoxications and public debaucheries were then by far the worst of this virago's shameless life. After the remnant of the popular army, which had reached the Wicklow mountains, was dispersed, she continued for some time with Holt. On her return home from the battle-field, she continued to speak at random of everything she saw or heard, and the more wicked the deed the more delight she took in the recital, and with a brutal pleasure exaggerating the atrocity. In a short time she was picked up by the ultra-loyalists, who liked to have her drinking in the public-houses with them, getting her to tell of the deeds she saw in civil war. It was only in the latter end of August she left the outlaw camp; and on the 16th of September she became the ward of Captain Wainright, the agent of Lord Fitzwilliam, the other magistrates of the county concurring in the project to have her for a general informer. She was then sent to Rathdrum, to be put under the training of a little vindictive and crafty attorney, named Tom King, and some old bailiffs.

She was now dressed like a lady, with habit and skirt, hat and feathers, and a prancing palfrey was placed at her disposal. In her excursions through the country, where she was often engaged in search of denounced men, or outlawed rebels, she presided at the head of a military party, which, it may be said, she actually commanded, for if they would not do as she wished, she swore that she would return to the garrison and not guide them any further. On one day she rode with a strong party to Ballymaurin, about three miles from Rathdrum, where two brothers, Byrne, were digging their own potatoes. Those men had been out fighting, but had returned home, like great numbers of others, and availed themselves of the Amnesty Act. She had some dislike to them; she pointed them out to her guards, and they were shot without more ado. Historic writers should be cautious in taking details from the papers of those days. The poor fellows that were shot, were called the 'Blacks', by nickname. After some excursions of a similar kind and some swearing of what was called a light nature, such as having men transported, or imprisoned for a considerable time, she was thought duly qualified to come forward to prosecute to the death. […]

DUNLAVIN GREEN

Anon.

In the year one thousand seven hundred and ninety-eight,
A sorrowful ditty to you I'm going to relate,
Concerning those heroes both clever and rare to be seen,
By false information were shot upon Dunlavin Green.

Woe to you, Saunders; disgrace me you never shall,
That the tears of the widows may melt you like snow before the sun;
Those fatherless orphans! their cries nor moans can't be screened,
For the loss of their fathers, who were shot upon Dunlavin Green.

Some of our heroes are 'listed and gone far away,
There are some of them dead, and some of them crossing the sea;
As for poor Andy Ryan, his mother distracted has been
For the loss of her son, who was shot upon Dunlavin Green.

As for Andy Farrell, I'm sure he has cause to complain,
And likewise the two Duffys, I'm sure they may well do the same;
Dwyer on the mountain to the Orange he owes a great spleen,
For the loss of his comrades, who were shot upon Dunlavin Green.

They were marched from the guard-house up to the end of the town,
And when they came there, the poor fellows were forced to kneel down;
Like lambs for the slaughter that day, it was plain to be seen;
Their blood ran in streams on the dykes of Dunlavin Green.

That we may live happy the joyful tidings to hear,
When we will have satisfaction for the murders they did in that year;
There were thirty-six heroes, both clever and rare to be seen,
Both loyal and united, shot one day on Dunlavin Green.

Now to conclude and finish my mournful tale,
I hope all good Christians to pray for their souls will not fail,
Their souls in white pigeons a-flying to heaven were seen,
On the very same day they were shot upon Dunlavin Green.

TWO POEMS

Mary Tighe

Dwyer and M'Alister
A Tale of 1798

Oft mid rebellion's blood-stained lines,
The noblest deeds of honour glow,
As the fair sun the brighter shines,
When storms around him darkness throw.

The outlaw in the cavern wild,
High o'er the still lake's smooth expanse,
Where rocks magnificently piled,
Conceal him from pursuer's glance

May still possess an heart that's form'd,
In brilliant honour's purest mould,
As softly by affection warmed,
As when in danger, stern and bold.

I sing M'Alister, the brave,
Whose deeds are worthy of a song;
To snatch them from oblivion's grave,
And bid them live both late and long.

M'Alister, the faithful friend,
Of him who waged th'unequal war,
And led his band from end to end,
Of Wicklow's mountains, famed afar.

The golden lure was held in vain,
The price of Dwyer's devoted head;
Nor hope of pardon or of gain,
An outlaw from his honour led.

Beset, pursued o'er hill and dell,
Through shady wood and rocky glen:
By murderous foes—ah! shame to tell,
For they themselves were highland-men.

From mountain-top to deepest vale,
Where caves conceal the chosen band;
Through the soft shades of dark Imail,
They hurl the dreadful fire-brand.

An hospitable roof remote,
Where whilome dwelt Glendalough's saint;
As evening's gentle vapours float,
Revived the outlaw weak and faint.

But still, the staunch hounds closely press,
To find their undiscovered haunt;
And by the tracks of blood they trace,
Those foes whom they could never daunt.

That blood had warmed the truest breast,
Ah! then, why was it idly shed?
It was to save their chief, distrest—
The blow was aimed at Dwyer's head.

M'Alister, with fury burning,
Received instead the deadly blow;
When quickly on the foeman turning,
The gallant chieftain laid him low.

Then o'er the wild heath swiftly bore,
His faint and wounded friend along,
And marked each step with trickling gore,
That on the heath-bells trembling hung.

And now within the peaceful cot,
Released from toil, as each suppose;
Refreshing rest they, wearied, sought,
And stretched themselves in soft repose.

When—hark! the bugle's thrilling blast,
Aroused them from their slumbers sweet;
Betrayed! they cried, come now, at last,
Like heroes we our death shall meet.

In crowds the kilted Scots surround
The outlaw'd rebel's calm retreat,
The cliffs with echoing shouts resound—
The valiant band for death await.

The flaming brand is tossed on high,
The crackling thatch now blazes wide—
The curling smoke ascends the sky—
The lake reflects her burning side.

The gallant band in mute despair,
Around their chosen leader stand;
Resolved in death his fate to share,
And nobly perish hand in hand.

Within they feel the scorching flame,
Abroad they dread the highland ball;
The polish'd bag'net's lightning gleam—
The blazing roof's destructive fall.

At length the solemn pause was broke.
M'Alister, in feeble tone,
His honour'd leader thus bespoke,
Whose life he prized beyond his own:

'The window which o'erhangs the deep,
A friendly passage opens wide;
'Tis but the rocky crag to leap,
To meet the still lake's dimpling tide.

Then gliding o'er the silvery wave,
To reach the shore each effort bend,
Whilst I the Scottish ruffians brave,
And sell my life to save my friend.

The thund'ring volley aimed at me,
A favouring moment will obtain:
Oh, snatch that moment and be free,
Nor let your friend's death be in vain.'

He said, and darted forth with speed,
Like arrow from the twanging bow;
Nor would his friend's remonstrance heed,
But rush'd to meet the deadly blow.

That instant roared the fatal peal;
Its flashes lit the mountain side;
The hero felt the leaden hail,
And like a hero nobly died.

Now forth the furious Dwyer sprung,
Along the craggy steep descent;
His valiant heart with anguish wrung—
His noble soul on vengeance bent;

Nor meanly sought his single life,
But stood exposed to Scottish view;
Resolved his death should end the strife,
Ere flames devour his faithful crew.

The Scotsmen turn to seize their prey,
And quickly take too certain aim;
Though wounded, still he stands at bay,
Until his band rush from the flame.

Then bounding o'er the rugged rock,
They safely reach the tangled wood;
Where thickest shades pursuers mock,
The grateful outlaws panting stood.

And now the pressing danger o'er,
They stretch along the blooming heath:
And each a solemn vengeance swore,
To take for their companion's death.

Lines Written at Rossana, November 18, 1799

Oh my rash hand! what hast thou idly done?
    Torn from its humble bank the last poor flower
    That patient lingered to this wintry hour:
Expanding cheerly to the languid sun
It flourished yet, and yet it might have blown,
    Had not thy sudden desolating power
    Destroyed what many a storm and angry shower
Had pitying spared. The pride of summer gone,
    Cherish what yet in faded life can bloom;
And if domestic love still sweetly smiles,
If sheltered by thy cot he yet beguiles
    Thy winter's prospect of its dreary gloom,
Oh, from the spoiler's touch thy treasure screen,
To bask beneath Contentment's beam serene!

from The Memoirs of Miles Byrne

Miles Byrne

It was during the stay our army made at the camp of Mount Pleasant, that poor Billy Byrne of Ballymanus by his humane interference saved the lives of several prisoners against whom charges of persecuting the people were brought. Amongst those prisoners was Thomas Dowse, a gentleman farmer and grazier, with whom poor Byrne was on intimate terms. Of course he used all his influence and succeeded in getting Dowse put at liberty. Could it be believed, that Dowse's evidence on Byrne's trial at Wicklow afterwards, in which he declared his heartfelt gratitude, and said, that to Byrne alone he owed his life, was the principal one on which the unfortunate Billy Byrne was found guilty and executed there. Byrne's influence with the insurgents, showing, he was a rebel to the British government.

At Mount Pleasant Byrne was in his own country and neighbourhood, where every one knew him and loved him and respected him; it was not extraordinary that he could save persons against whom no very serious crimes were proved, still this humane act sufficed to the cruel ascendancy men who conducted the trial at Wicklow, to show that Byrne must have been a chief, or he would not have had the power to save Thomas Dowse from being put to death. How monstrous, and how lamentable to have so fine a fellow sacrificed, to appease the thirst of the Orange blood hounds!

Brigade Major Fitzgerald of General Hunter's staff at Wexford, procured for Byrne a protection from the general in chief of the English forces there; on the faith of which protection, he quitted the country and came to Dublin to join his sisters. There he had been publicly walking about for more than a month previous to his arrest, so conscious was he of his innocence and that he had nothing to apprehend. Particularly as his elder brother Garrett Byrne, who was one of the principal leaders and distinguished generals of our Irish army, had surrendered some time before to Sir John Moore on condition of being allowed to quit the country and expatriate himself forever. What a pity that William Byrne had not to do with a man like John Moore, who valued his own word of honour and his reputation, pledged to Garrett Byrne more than any flattery or reward he could obtain from the castle inquisitors who presided over the destinies of the unfortunate country at that memorable epoch in the city of Dublin.

I trust it may not be thought presumption in me to say so much on this sad subject, but though very young at the time, I knew poor Byrne too well not to appreciate his high mind, and the horror with which he spoke of crimes committed previous to, and during the insurrection. I dined beside him two days before his arrest, at the house of my half-brother Edward Kennedy. I came from my hiding place to meet him there, and could not help observing the serenity of his manner and the great security he felt, that no danger could await him, in consequence of the protection he had obtained.

Alas! he was soon cruelly undeceived and taught that no reliance could be placed on the protection granted the authorization of the cold-hearted Lord Cornwallis, or of any of the English tyrants then ruling over unhappy Ireland.

Byrne's sudden trial and execution at Wicklow caused the most sorrowful sensation throughout the country and saddened the hearts of all those to whom he was personally known. He was a perfect gentleman, with the soundest understanding. He evinced the greatest courage. He was amiable and simple in his manners; handsome, powerful strong and well-proportioned; six feet six inches in height, about 24 years of age. Such was the ever to be lamented Billy Byrne.

BILLY BYRNE OF BALLYMANUS

Anon.

Come all ye brave United Men, I pray you lend an ear,
And listen to these verses I now will let you hear,
Concerning Billy Byrne, a man of great renown,
Who was tried and hanged at Wicklow town, a traitor to the Crown.

It was in the year of ninety-eight, we got reason to complain,
We lost our brave commander, Billy Byrne was his name;
He was taken in Dublin city and brought to Wicklow jail,
And though we wished to free him, for him they'd take no bail.

When he was taken prisoner the lot against him swore
That he a Captain's title upon Mount Pleasant bore,
Before the King's grand army his men he did review
And with a piece of cannon marched on for Carrigrua.

And when the trial was started the informers they came in
There was Dixon, Doyle and Davis and likewise Bid Doolin
They thought it little scruple his precious blood to spill
Who never robbed nor murdered nor to any man did ill.

It would melt your heart with pity how these traitors did explain
That Byrne worked the cannon on Arklow's bloody plain,
They swore he was committed to support the United cause,
The Judge he cried out: 'Guilty', to be hanged by coercion laws.

One of those prosecutors, I often heard him tell,
It was at his father's table he was often treated well,
And in his brother's kitchen where many did he see,
The Byrnes were well rewarded for their civility.

My curse light on you Dixon, I ne'er will curse your soul,
It was at the Bench at Wicklow you swore without control,
The making of a false oath you thought it a little sin,
To deprive the County Wicklow of the flower of all its men.

Where are you, Mathew Davis, or why don't you come on,
To prosecute the prisoner who now lies in Rathdrum?
The devil has him chained repenting for his sins,
In lakes of fire and brimstone and sulphur to the chin.

When the devil saw him coming he sang a merry song,
Saying: 'You're welcome, Mathew Davis! What kept you out so long?
Where is that traitor, Dixon, to the crown so loyal and true?
I have a warm corner for him and, of course, Bid Doolin, too.'

Success to Billy Byrne! May his name forever shine
Through Wicklow, Wexford and Kildare and all along the line,
May the Lord have mercy on his soul and all such souls as he,
Who stand up straight for Ireland's cause and die for Liberty!

ANNE DEVLIN'S LAMENT FOR EMMET

Ethna Carbery

My heart's blood was yours, my love was the same,
And would my soul had flown to God before the trouble came,
Ah, would I were there to slumber within the narrow bed,
And you in youth and glory were marching overhead.
Mobouchal dheas, 'tis lonely and old now am I,
Around me the shadows all day darkly lie,
My weary nights are haunted by dreams, 'Mhuire's truagh!
Of the sweet maid whose loving heart broke for love of you.
On the brown heathery hills no danger lurked I ween,
With Wicklowmen to guard you, and pikes bristling keen,
But her eyes drew you forth from their sheltering care,
For a kiss from her red lips, a curl from her hair.
The rose left her cheek, the brave eyes grew dim,
She drained the bitter cup of sorrow to the brim.

When that sad September moon saw your young head lie low,
And the dawn of Ireland shrouded in a dark cloud of woe,
I had died for you gladly, my courage never quailed,
When their swords pierced my bosom, their wild threats assailed.
Nor did their prison torture win from me a single tear,
That memory of grief and pain would fade if you were here.
May Christ give you peace in your nameless biding-place,
Sleep soft, my withered flower, nor weep for our disgrace,
The Mother bows beneath her chains, her dear harp-song is dumb,
She pines among her sighing reeds until a victor come.
Oh! had the cruel spoiler spared your young dark head,
The tramp of your United hosts had waked the very dead.
The shouts of your triumph had thundered to the sky,
But alas! and alas in the cold grave you lie.

TWO POEMS

John Millington Synge

QUEENS

Seven dog-days we let pass
Naming Queens in Glenmacnass
All the rare and royal names
Wormy sheepskin yet retains:
Etain, Helen, Maeve, and Fand,
Golden Deirdre's tender hand;
Bert, the big-foot, sung by Villon.
Cassandra, Ronsard found in Lyon.
Queens of Sheba, Meath, and Connaught.
Coifed with crown, or gaudy bonnet;
Queens whose finger once did stir men,
Queens were eaten of fleas and vermin,
Queens men drew like Mona Lisa,
Or slew with drugs in Rome and Pisa.
We named Lucrezia Crivelli,
And Titian's lady with amber belly,
Queens acquainted in learned sin,
Jane of Jewry's slender shin:
Queens who cut the boss of Glanna,
Judith of Scripture, and Gloriana,
Queens who wasted the East by proxy,
Or drove the ass-cart, a tinker's doxy.
Yet these are rotten—I ask their pardon—
And we've the sun on rock and garden;
These are rotten, so you're the Queen
Of all are living, or have been.

A QUESTION

I asked if I got sick and died, would you
With my black funeral go walking too,
If you'd stand close to hear them talk or pray
While I'm let down in that steep bank of clay.

And, No, you said, for if you saw a crew
Of living idiots pressing round that new
Oak coffin—they alive, I dead beneath
That board—you'd rave and rend them with your teeth.

FROM JERUSALEM

William Blake

PLATE 49

Jerusalem! Jerusalem! why wilt thou turn away?
Come ye, O Daughters of Beulah, lament for Og & Sihon
Upon the Lakes of Ireland from Rathlin to Baltimore.
Stand ye upon the Dargle from Wicklow to Drogheda...

THE SUGARLOAF: LUNAR ECLIPSE WITH A COMET*

Mark Granier

The car's cooling engine
ticks. Cows cough
in the dark fields nearby.

Occasional headlights
flare up and fan past us,
sealing the silence.

Others are here, parked
at discreet distances.
This is the place

to watch a discolouring moon,
sepia now
in our planetary shadow.

Beyond it, that micro-speck
(indistinguishable, stuck-fast
near the frozen Plough)

is a mountain flaming past,
missing us by a mere
9 million miles…

Without charts or telescopes
it's pointless.
So we settle for

half an hour, standing about
or lying on our backs
on the car-bonnet;

letting our bare-faced gaze
skid across the ice-black
primordial lid, and listening,

listening, listening…

---

* *Not our recent familiar, the highly visible Hale Bopp, but the much less spectacular Hyakutake of 1996.*

FROM PERSONAL SKETCHES AND RECOLLECTIONS

Jonah Barrington

The scenery of Wicklow is doubtless on a very minor scale, quite unable to compete with the grandeur and immensity of continental landscape. Even to our own Killarney it is not comparable; but it possesses a genial, glowing luxury, whereof more elevated scenery is often destitute. It is, besides, in the world; its beauties seem alive. It blooms, it blossoms: the mellow climate extracts from every shrub a tribute of fragrance wherewith the atmosphere is saturated, and through such a medium does the refreshing rain descend to brighten the hues of the evergreens!

I frankly admit myself an enthusiast as to that lovely district. In truth, I fear I should have been enthusiastic on many points, had not law, the most powerful antidote to that feeling, interposed to check its growth.

The site of my sylvan residence, Dunran, was nearly in the centre of the golden belt, about fifteen miles from the capital; but owing to the varied nature of the country, it appeared far more distant. Bounded by the beautiful glen of the Downs, at the foot of the magnificent Bellevue, and the more distant sugar-loaf mountain called the Dangle, together with Tynnehinch—less celebrated for its unrivalled scenery than as the residence of Ireland's first patriot—the dark, deep glen, the black lake, and mystic vale of Lugelough, contrasted quite magically with the highly cultivated beauties of Dunran—the parks and wilds, and sublime cascade of Powerscourt, and the newly-created magnificence of Mount Kennedy, abundantly prove that perfection itself may exist in contrasts. In fine, I found myself enveloped by the hundred beauties of that enchanting district, which, though of one family, were rendered yet more attractive by the variety of their features; and had I not been tied to laborious duties, I should infallibly have sought refuge there altogether from the care of the world.

One of the greatest pleasures I enjoyed whilst resident at Dunran was the near abode of the late Lord Rossmore, at that time commander-in-chief in Ireland. His lordship knew my father, and from my commencement in public life had been my friend, and a sincere one. He was a Scotsman born, but had come to Ireland when very young, as page to the Lord-Lieutenant. He had married an heiress, had purchased the estate of

Mount Kennedy, built a noble mansion, laid out some of the finest gardens in Ireland, and in fact improved the demesne as far as taste, skill, and money could accomplish. He was what may be called a remarkably fine old man, quite the gentleman, and when at Mount Kennedy quite the *country* gentleman. He lived in a style few people can attain to: his table, supplied by his own farms, was adapted to the Viceroy himself, yet was ever spread for his neighbours; in a word, no man was ever better repaid by universal esteem. Had his connexions possessed his understanding, and practised his habits, they would probably have found more friends when they wanted them.

The intimacy at Mount Kennedy gave rise to an occurrence the most extraordinary and inexplicable of my whole existence, an occurrence which for many years occupied my thoughts and wrought on my imagination. Lord Rossmore was advanced in years, but I never heard of his having had a single day's indisposition. He bore in his green old age the appearance of robust health. During the viceroyalty of Earl Hardwick, Lady Barrington, at a drawing-room at Dublin Castle, met Lord Rossmore. He had been making up one of his weekly parties for Mount Kennedy, to commence the next day, and had sent down orders for every preparation to be made. The Lord-Lieutenant was to be of the company.

'My little farmer,' said he to Lady Barrington, addressing her by a pet name, 'when you go home, tell Sir Jonah that no business is to prevent him from bringing you down to dine with me to-morrow. I will have no *ifs* in the matter—so tell him that come he *must!*' She promised positively, and on her return informed me of her engagement, to which I at once agreed. We retired to our chamber about twelve, and towards two in the morning I was awakened by a sound of a very extraordinary nature. I listened; it occurred first at short intervals, it resembled neither a voice nor an instrument, it was softer than any voice, and wilder than any music, and seemed to float in the air. I don't know wherefore, but my heart beat forcibly; the sound became still more plaintive, till it almost died away in the air, when a sudden change, as if excited by a pang changed its tone; it seemed *descending*. I felt every nerve tremble: it was not a *natural* sound, nor could I make out the point from whence it came.

At length I awakened Lady Barrington, who heard it as well as myself; she suggested that it might be an Eolian harp; but to that instrument it bore no similitude—it was altogether a different *character of sound*. My wife at first appeared less affected than I, but subsequently she was more so.

We now went to a large window in our bed-room which looked

directly upon a small garden underneath; the sound seemed then obviously to ascend from a grass-plot immediately below our window. It continued; Lady Barrington requested that I would call up her maid, which I had, and she was evidently more affected than either of us. The sounds lasted for more than half an hour. At last a deep, heavy, throbbing sigh seemed to issue from the spot, and was shortly succeeded by a sharp but low cry, and the distinct exclamation, thrice repeated of 'Rossmore—Rossmore—Rossmore!' I will not attempt to describe my own feelings, indeed I cannot. The maid fled in terror from the window, and it was with difficulty I prevailed on Lady Barrington to return to bed; in about a minute after, the sound died gradually away until all was silent.

Lady Barrington, who is not so *superstitious* as I, attributed this circumstance to a hundred different causes, and made me promise that I would not mention it next day in Mount Kennedy, since we should be thereby rendered *laughingstock*. At length, wearied with speculation, we fell into a sound slumber.

About seven the ensuing morning a strong rap at my chamber-door awakened me. The recollection of the past night's adventure rushed immediately upon my mind, and rendered me very unfit to be taken suddenly on any subject. It was light; I went to the door, when my faithful servant, Lawler, exclaimed on the other side, 'O Lord sir!' 'What is the matter?' said I hurriedly, 'O sir!' ejaculated he, 'Lord Rossmore's footman was running past the door in great haste, and told me in passing that my lord, after coming from the castle, had gone to bed in perfect health, but that about *half-after two* this morning his own man hearing a noise in his master's bed—he slept in the same room—went to him, and found him in the agonies of death, and before he could alarm the other servants all was over!'

I conjecture nothing. I only relate the incident as unequivocally matter of *fact*. Lord Rossmore was *absolutely dying at the moment I heard his name pronounced*. Let sceptics draw their own conclusions; perhaps natural causes *may* be assigned; but *I* am totally unequal to the task.

Atheism may ridicule me, Orthodoxy may despise me, Bigotry may lecture me, Fanaticism may *burn* me, yet in my very faith I would seek consolation. It is, in my mind, better to believe *too much* than *too little*, and that is the only theological crime of which I can be fairly accused.

FROM THE IRISH SKETCH BOOK

William Thackeray

All the hills up which we had panted had imparted a fierce sensation of hunger; and it was nobly decreed that we should stop in the middle of the street of Roundwood, impartially between the two hotels, and solemnly decide upon a resting-place after having inspected the larders and bedrooms of each.

And here, as an impartial writer, I must say that the hotel of Mr Wheatly possesses attractions which few men can resist, in the shape of two very handsome young ladies his daughters; whose faces, were they but painted on his signboard, instead of the mysterious piece which ornaments it, would infallibly draw tourists into the house, thereby giving the opposition inn of Murphy not the least chance of custom.

A landlord's daughters in England, inhabiting a little country inn, would be apt to lay the cloth for the traveller, and their respected father would bring in the first dish of the dinner; but this arrangement is never known in Ireland: we scarcely ever see the cheering countenance of my landlord. And as for the young ladies of Roundwood, I am bound to say that no young person in Baker Street could be more genteel; and that our bill, when it was brought the next morning, was written in as pretty and fashionable a lady's hand as ever was formed in the most elegant finishing school at Pimlico.

Of the dozen houses of the little village, the half seem to be houses of entertainment. A green common stretches before these, with its rural accompaniments of geese, pigs, and idlers; a park and plantation at the end of the village, and plenty of trees round about it, give it a happy, comfortable, English look; which is, to my notion, the best compliment that can be paid to a hamlet: for where, after all, are villages so pretty?

Here, rather to one's wonder—for the district was not thickly enough populated to encourage dramatic exhibitions—a sort of theatre was erected on the common, a ragged cloth covering the spectators and the actors, and the former (if there were any) obtaining admittance through two doors on the stage in front, marked 'Pit & Galery'. Why should the word not be spelt with one l as with two?

The entrance to the 'pit' was stated to be threepence, and to the 'galery' twopence. We heard the drums and pipes of the orchestra as we sat at dinner: it seemed to be a good opportunity to examine Irish humour of a peculiar sort, and we promised ourselves a pleasant evening in the pit.

But although the drums began to beat at half-past six, and a crowd of young people formed round the ladder at that hour, to whom the manager of the troop addressed the most vehement invitations to enter, nobody seemed to be inclined to mount the steps: for the fact most likely was, that not one of the poor fellows possessed the requisite twopence which would induce the fat old lady who sat by it to fling open the gallery door. At once I thought of offering a half-crown for a purchase of tickets for twenty, and so at once benefiting the manager and crowd of ragged urchins who stood wistfully without his pavilion; but it seemed ostentatious, and we had not the courage to face the tall man in the great-coat gesticulating and shouting in front of the stage, and make the proposition.

Why not? It would have given the company potatoes at least for supper, and made a score of children happy. They would have seen 'the learned pig who spells your name, the feats of manly activity, the wonderful Italian vaulting', and they would have heard the comic songs by 'your humble servant'.

'Your humble servant' was the head of the troop: a long man, with a broad accent, a yellow top-coat, and a piteous lean face. What a speculation was this poor fellow's! He must have a company of at least a dozen to keep. There were three girls in trousers, who danced in front of the stage, in Polish caps, tossing their arms about to the tunes of three musicianers; there was a page, two young tragedy-actors, and a clown; there was the fat old woman at the gallery-door waiting for the twopences; there was the Jack Pudding; and it was evident that there must have been someone within, or else who would take care of the learned pig?

The poor manager stood in front, and shouted to the little Irishry beneath; but no one seemed to move. Then he brought forward Jack Pudding, and had a dialogue with him; the jocularity of which, by heavens! made the heart ache to hear. We had determined, at least, to go to the play before that, but the dialogue was too much: we were obliged to walk away, unable to face that dreadful Jack Pudding, and heard the poor manager shouting still for many hours through the night, and the drums thumping vain invitations to the people. O unhappy children of the Hibernian Thespis! It is my belief that they must have eaten the learned pig that night for supper.

FROM IRELAND, ITS SCENERY, CHARACTER, &c.

Mr and Mrs Hall

About two miles from the inn at Newarth Bridge, and one from the village of Ashford, commences the entrance to 'The Devil's Glen', or rather to that side of it which is the property of Charles Tottenham, Esq.; for the river divides it; the opposite land belonging to Francis Synge, Esq. Mr Tottenham requires that all visitors shall leave their names at his Lodge, where an order for admission into the glen is given by the gate-keeper, a kindly and gossiping dame, in whose company the stranger may spend a few minutes very profitably. A narrow road—but not too narrow for ordinary carriages—shadowed all the way by luxuriant trees, runs, for nearly a mile, to the iron gate that bars the passage of all intruders; but where a call for admission is at once answered. As we enter (the overhanging foliage has hitherto concealed its character), the scene that at once bursts upon the sight is inconceivably grand and beautiful. We are between two huge mountains, the precipitous sides of the one being covered with the finest forest trees, of innumerable forms and hues, the greater number having been planted by the hand of Nature; but where she had manifested neglect or indifference, Art has acted as a skilful and judicious attendant, and provided a remedy for the omission. The other mountain is rugged and half-naked; huge masses of uncovered stone jutting out over the brawling river, into which they seem to fall, and where gigantic rocks have already striven to stay the onward progress of the wrathful current—in vain. How striking and how exquisite is the contrast between the side rich in foliage, and that which still continues here! for

> 'Green leaves were here:
> But 'twas the foliage of the rocks, the birch,
> The yew, the holly, and the bright green thorn,
> With hanging islands of resplendent furze.'

while between both, at a prodigious depth below their summits, rushes the rapid river, brawling so loudly as to drown the music of the birds; now a mass of foam, now subsiding into a calm miniature lake, where the trout find rest, and where the water is so clear that you may count the silver fins beneath it. The glen is little more than a mile in length; and midway a small moss-house has been erected; to our minds, the structure—although exceedingly simple—disturbed the perfect solitude of the place; where the work of the artificer ought not to be recognised. But this evil is insignificant compared to one, of very recent origin, against which we may justly enter our protest—a wide carriage road has been constructed all through the glen; stolen partly from the river's bed, and partly from the mountain's base! Alas for the sylphs and dryads who have had their dwelling here! Alas for those who love untouched and untainted nature! Let us hope that the river, exasperated beyond control, will avenge itself upon the insolent engineer, who sought to restrain a mountain torrent within 'licensed bounds'. And this result is, indeed, to be looked for; the waterfall at the head of the glen, that dances so joyously and so 'orderly' in summer, must be, in winter, a mighty cataract, full of fury, that no barrier, the work of man, can be expected to withstand.

Nothing in the county of Wicklow astonished us, or gratified us, so much as the Devil's Glen; with its roaring river, its huge precipices, its circuitous paths, and the noble and graceful 'fall,' that seems as a crown of glory to its head. It is impossible for language to convey a notion of our delight, when we had climbed the mountain steep—by the tangled footway that ascends from the moss-house—and gazed below and around us. It is perhaps the most graceful, if not the most stupendous, of the Wicklow cataracts; it comes rushing and roaring down from the heights above, between rocks, through which it would seem to have a channel; then, as elsewhere, pausing awhile as if to gather a sufficient force with which to move onwards; and then dashing aside every impediment that would bar its progress to the sea.

Reader, to reach it is, literally, but a day's journey from London!

FROM STANDING AT THE CROSSROADS

Phil O'Keeffe

Our family tree was rooted deep in the soil of West Wicklow. My father was one of a family of seven sons and three daughters from the small hilly town of Tinahely where my Grandfather Crowley ran a small bakery; my mother was the only child of Johnny Whitty and Elizabeth O'Neill of Kyle, Ballinglen, who married and settled in Dublin where Grandfather Whitty was employed as a drayman with Guinness's brewery. Our two 'aunts', Aunt Mary Keenan who lived in a small farm just above my great-grandfather's old home, and Aunt Nanny Keenan who lived at Three Wells above Aughrim, were really my mother's first cousins. They were married to two brothers, and most of our cousins were older than we were. The pull of Wicklow was immensely strong and drew us back year after year when the long summer holidays were upon us. This year I was going to go there on my own, on my first holiday from work.

That week of my adult holiday was a good one. I wandered on my own over the brow of the hill and along the back road to the town of Aughrim; I heard the swish, swish, swish of the narrow ribbon of milk as it hit the bottom of the can held between Uncle Dan's knees and I tried with inexperienced fingers to coax milk from Bessie the cow, who rolled frightened eyes at me as I sat unsteadily on the little three-cornered stool. I carried water from the only one of the Three Wells used for human consumption, dipping the bucket expertly into the cool recess, balancing it on the shiny flags, perpetually wet with water drawn for half a dozen homes, and leaning well to the right as I carried the bucket of sparkling water home to the house.

In the evenings when the cows had been milked and the fowl, the pigs and the calves had been fed and bedded and the fading day had yielded to the gentle night, Mary, Liam and I walked to the wells in our light shoes, the heavy working shoes discarded by the kitchen door. Neighbours gathered for a chat, to quietly discuss the day's doings and make plans for winter sowing, fencing, snagging turnips and dipping sheep. As the fat toads croaked in the damp growth beside the wells, we laughed and talked while the crickets chirped and the rabbits on the rise of the hill were etched against the lingering evening sky.

We had laid my father to rest the previous summer in the graveyard above Tinahely, and during the week in Aughrim I cycled with Liam the seven miles to Kyle to visit Aunt Mary and to take part in the preparations for the pattern, the annual ceremony of blessing the graves. After we cleaned and tidied the graves and I traced my father's name where it had been newly added to the gravestone of my grandparents, I sat back on my heels, closed my eyes and remembered. Every year we had gone back for the pattern. The train from Dublin to Shillelagh left Westland Row at twenty-five to seven on the Sunday morning. With Madge and Babs in charge, Betty, Tess and I set out at twenty-five to six from our home. My father and mother, with Nance in the go-car, followed behind, giving us a five-minute start. Madge calculated that if we were at the Holy Faith Convent on the Coombe when their chapel bell called out the morning Angelus, then we would be in time for the train.

At Westland Row we sat on the station seats and drank milk from the bottles which my mother had packed at the back of Nance's go-car. I loved the hustle of the railway station, with trains shunting back and forth spewing cascades of steam and raining soft, insinuating coal-dust. I loved the sound of the guardsman's whistle clamped between his teeth, and watching the red flag raised in his hand as he waited for the latecomers rushing past the ticket-collector's hut. With pennies clutched in our hands we made for the name-plate machine where we punched our names and addresses onto pieces of tin. We swung the big iron handle through the letters of the alphabet, made mistakes, corrected them and swung again. As we waited for the train to Shillelagh we read aloud the captions under the huge advertisements; we laughed at the two faces of the Mac's Smile blades, and at the dopey man in the Andrews Liver Salts who searched through his case for the all-important tin which was peeping from the pocket of his sprawling posterior and who perplexedly mouthed the words, 'I must have left it behind'. And we always chanted the advertisement for the Waverly pen:

> 'It came as a boon and a blessing to men.
> Pickwick the Owl and the Waverly pen.'

From Westland Row to Woodenbridge we all dozed, waking in time to change trains to Kilcommon, below Funeral Hill, where we stumbled from the train to breathe good, fresh country air. The smell from turf-fires as the smoke rose lazily in the stillness of morning was like heady perfume for me. We were well in time for the second Mass, and then my mother and father spent the rest of the morning and early afternoon painting the kerbs of the family's graves while we helped pull weeds and water flowers. My great-grandmother's iron cross had been cast at the Hammond Lane foundry in Dublin, and when we found it my mother would once again say, 'Your great-grandmother, God be good to her, she survived the famine, you know.'

It was my father's pride to walk the street of his beloved home town and introduce his family to those he met, and our welcome was always warm and strong. Tired and happy with work well done, and the pattern for one more year dutifully attended to, and 'God bless' and 'God go with you' and 'God give you a safe journey home' echoing in our ears, we sat contentedly on the green garden benches of the little railway station, pictures of white-washed cottages and stacks of dark brown turf still fresh in our minds.

STILL LIFE

Sylvia Bowe

The sound of weeping came clearly to Veronica as she dozed in her chair by the fire. For a moment, she felt disoriented, not sure where she was. Then her vision cleared as much as it ever did now, and she realized the heart-wrenching sound was coming from the next room, Laura's room.

It took her several minutes to rise from the deep arm-chair with the aid of her stick and make her way to the door. Laura opened the door at the first tap, the sight of her giving Veronica's heart a painful squeeze, the usually pretty face swollen and bruised from crying.

'Don't tell me. Let me guess. It has to be a man,' Veronica said.

'He said he didn't want to see me anymore. He said we should see other people.'

This last word turned into a loud wail amid a fresh flood of tears. Veronica bundled her into the room and closed the door.

'Shush! Do you want your mother up here? You know what she's like. She'll send me to my room and you'll get The Lecture.'

Veronica mimicked Edel's rather high-pitched, grand accent. 'You're not the only one with problems, you know. Look at all the poor people starving in Africa.'

A snort of laughter bubbled out from under the sodden tissue Laura held to her face.

'That's better. Now, tell me all about it.'

Taking Laura's hand, Veronica lowered herself gingerly onto the edge of the bed.

'There's not much to tell, really. It's over. It's over because Mike says it's over. Two years, seven months and sixteen days we've been together. How could he do this to me? I can't go on without him, Gran!'

The sobs came again. Veronica knew she would have to choose her words carefully. She spoke very gently.

'Laura, you're only nineteen, you've got your whole life ahead of you. I know you feel now that you'll never get over this, but you will. Believe me. In time you'll meet someone else…'

Laura leapt to her feet, eyes blazing.

'Can you hear yourself?' she said in a tight angry voice. '"You'll meet someone else", "You'll get over it." You can't possibly understand how I feel.'

The words tumbled out of Veronica's mouth before she could stop them.

'Oh, but I do understand. More than you know. I wasn't always the old woman you see here, you know. I was once young, as you are now, my hair was dark like yours and I wore it round my shoulders in big, soft curls…'

Laura had stopped crying and looked at Veronica in surprise. Veronica rarely, if ever, spoke about herself and her life, except in general terms, like: 'We never had a choice about what to have for our dinner in my day. It was take it or leave it.' But this was new.

'Go on, Gran,' Laura said softly.

'Oh, you don't want to hear about all that. Ancient history,' Veronica blustered.

'Oh, but I do. Please.'

Veronica looked closely at the girl's face for a long moment, seeming to weigh something up in her mind, and finally nodded curtly before speaking.

'Right, here goes. May as well tell someone my life story before I die.' She flashed a quick smile.

'I was seventeen years old, a grown woman in those days, and I'd been working in Duffy's Drapers in town for two years. I liked it there; the girls were nice, it was warm in the shop and the manager, Mr Byrne, was decent enough. Every Saturday night, me and my friend Agnes would go out dancing, usually to The Royal, that was our favourite because they had lovely toilets there. So when Agnes' eighteenth birthday fell on a Saturday, we decided we'd go to The Royal that night to celebrate. I remember I wore a powder blue dress with a navy belt, and a ribbon in my hair to match.

'To cut a long story short, I met someone that night who came to mean a great deal to me. So much so, that when he went away, I too thought that I would die from missing him. But as you can see I'm still here, so no matter how bad it feels at the time, a broken heart is not fatal.'

She stopped. Laura protested. 'You're not going to stop there, are you?' Then in a gentler tone, 'Please. Tell me what happened.'

Veronica sighed, fixed her eyes on a distant place, and took a deep breath.

'His name was Billy, he was twenty years old and a fitter with the Gas Company. He had brown wavy hair, a bit too long, blue eyes, was tall and skinny, nothing to write home about, I suppose, but as soon as I saw him I thought he was gorgeous. We danced together all that night, and when he walked me home, he asked me out to the pictures. After that, we were going steady, and I could think of nothing else, day or night, but my Billy.

'I loved everything about him. The bump on his nose, the way his eyebrows met slightly in the middle, his long eyelashes, and most of all the way his hands like big, gentle paws held my face up to be kissed. We had it bad. Sitting on a bench in the park, gazing into each other's eyes as if we were the only two people in the world. We would go for walks, miles and miles, holding hands, talking, or just happy to be together. Everyone took it for granted that we were a couple and that was that.

'But I had a secret. Not even Billy knew this secret, so ashamed of it was I. You see, I lusted for him. Sometimes I couldn't bear to look at the shape of his body through the white shirts he wore in the summer. I would turn my head in case he'd see the desire on my face. I knew it was wrong, but I couldn't help it. It was wrong and oh…so…wonderful!

'I wanted to reach out and touch the smooth golden skin of him, press my lips to the tiny beads of sweat shimmering on his neck. But how could I? Women never spoke of such things. Men probably didn't say a whole lot, either. I had never heard anyone speak of feelings like this. But, inevitably, nature took its course and words were unnecessary. It was a day trip to the Pine Forest and I was nineteen by then. We were surrounded by tall trees and the smell of the pines was stinging my nose. The needles lay deep and soft on the ground, the sunlight fell in moving patterns through the dark green branches. We made love for the first time in that forest, and I thought that I would surely die from the passion of it. When I went home I was sure my mother would be able to tell by looking at my face. But no one noticed anything, and life went on as before.

'Well, not quite as before. We were on fire for each other and took every chance we could get to be alone. Not every time was as romantic as the first in that idyllic setting, but I didn't care as long as I could touch him, feel him, love him. I dreamed that soon we would be married and it would be our secret life until then. Months later, when my twenty-first birthday came round, I was sure I'd get an engagement ring. But nothing happened, and I was so upset and embarrassed in front of my family, that later when we were alone I plucked up the courage to ask him why. I'll never forget what he said. He shuffled his feet for a minute and looked down at the floor. "I don't know how to say this. I've been trying to tell you for ages. I'm not ready to get married."

'I knew there was more; I knew by the blushing red colour of his face, the way he wouldn't look me in the eye. Eventually he blurted it out. "I just don't love you any more, Ronnie. I'm sorry." Just like that. I was sure there was some mistake. How could I not have known? I threw him out of the house, told him I never wanted to see him again. He left, not too reluctantly, I noticed. I locked myself in my room and cried, as you are crying now. I thought, "I will never love anyone else as long as I live." I was wrong. In time I picked up the pieces and went back to work, back to my friends and the usual round of social events; parties, dances, funerals, christenings… but not weddings. It was a long time before I could face that.

'Anyway, over the years, one by one my friends got married, then my younger sister Brenda, until I was the old maid of the family, on the shelf at 28 years of age, "Disappointed in Love." So you can imagine the shock when I came home from work one day and announced that I was getting married. To Mr Byrne, Albert, my boss for nearly fifteen years. He was twenty years older than me, but I knew he'd make a good husband. And he did. We had thirty happy years together, and I loved him for it. He loved me, too, in his own way. I miss him, your Grandad.'

Veronica blinked hard, as if waking from a dream.

'Anyway, I didn't mean to go on so long. This is between the two of us, do you hear me now? Your mother'd have a field day with this if she heard. Now, dry your eyes and go wash your face.'

'But Gran, what happened to Billy?'

'I never saw him again. He probably got married like I did and had a houseful of children. I just hope he had as good a life as I've had.'

'I think he was a fool to walk away from you. You were too good for him.'

For an instant Veronica was dismayed at the brittle tone of Laura's voice. 'Oh God, she's so like me,' she thought. Out loud she said briskly, 'Well, nearly time for tea. Come on, up you get. I'm going to run a comb through my hair and I'll be down in a minute.' She rose from the bed. Laura kissed her cheek and smiled. Not her old smile, but making a brave attempt. 'Good girl,' Veronica said, patting her hand.

In her own room again, Veronica opened a drawer and, instead of a comb, drew out an old yellowing photograph of a lanky young man leaning on the bonnet of an old Ford and smiling happily at the world. A quotation she had read many years before came to her mind. 'Most men lead lives of quiet desperation.' 'Most women too, I bet,' she murmured.

The world was a hard place for women, she knew. If she was lucky, Laura would escape the fate that had befallen Veronica.

But only if she was lucky.

A single tear escaped and ran down her wrinkled cheek, to be wiped away as so many others had been. She put the picture away.

As she bustled around the room, preparing to face her daughter over the tea-table, Veronica glanced in the mirror and smiled. Fine. Everything as it should be. Let the battle commence.

And as she descended the stairs at a fairly brisk pace, every step echoed in her mind, as every heartbeat had echoed in it for fifty years, 'Billy, Billy, Billy, where are you Billy…'

LAMENT FOR CEARBHALL Ó DÁLAIGH

Paul Durcan

Into a simple grave six feet deep,
Next grave to a Kerry sheep farmer,
Your plain oak coffin was laid
In a hail of hail:
The gods in the Macgillycuddy's Reeks
(Snow on their summits)
Were in a white, dancing rage
Together with the two don-
Keys who would not budge
From the graveyard.
And the poets and the painters,
The actors and the actresses,
The etchers and the sculptors,
The child-singers—those multiplying few
Who, despite the ever-darkening night,
Believe with their hearts' might
As did you
In a spoken music of the utter earth:

You who, for a brief hour,
Were Chieftain of a Rising People;
Who brought back into Tara's Halls
The blind poets and the blinder harpists;
Who, the brief hour barely ended,
Were insulted massively,
Betrayed
By a sanctimonious bourgeoisie;
And, worse by far,
By *la trahison des clercs;*
Where were those talented men
In the government of the talents
When the jackbooted
Bourgeois crackled the whip?

The talented men kept their silence,
Their souls committed to finance;
Now hear their mouth-traps snap shut:
'No comment, no comment, no comment, no comment.'
Ah, Cearbhall, but in your death
You led them all a merry dance:
Hauling them all out of their soft Dublin haunts,
Out of their Slickness and Glickness,
Out of their Snugvilles and Smugtowns,
You had them travel all the long,
Long way down to Sneem:
Sneem of the Beautiful Knot:
By God, and by Dana,
Cearbhall, forgive me
But it was a joy to watch them
With their wind-flayed faces
Getting all knotted-up
In the knot of your funeral;
Wind, rain, hail, and sleet,
Were on your side;
And spears of sunlight
Who, like yourself, did not lie;
Blue Lightning,
Gold Thunder.

In all our memories, Cearbhall,
You will remain as fresh
As the green rock jutting up
In mid-stream
Where fresh and salt waters meet
Under the Bridge at Sneem.

How the respectability squirmed
In the church when beside your coffin
The Ó Riada choir sang pagan laments
For their dead chieftain:
'O he is my hero, my brave loved one.'
Papal Nuncio, bishops, monsignori,

Passed wind in their misericords,
Their stony faces expressionless.
A Gaelic Chinaman whose birthplace
At 85 Main Street, Bray,
Is today a Chinese Restaurant
(The Jasmine, owned by Chi Leung Nam);
O tan-man smiling on the mountain,
You are gone from us now, O Yellow Sun:
Small laughing man,
Cearbhall of the merry eyes,
A Gaelic Charlie Chaplin who became
Chief Justice and President,
Hear our mute confessions now:
We were afraid of the man that licks
Life with such relish;
We were not up to your tricks,
Did not deserve you, Cearbhall
Of the City-Centre and the Mountain-Pool:
Príomh Breitheamh, Uachtarán: Slán.

March 1978

WALL OF DEATH, BRAY

Fergus Allen

Lashing out with my celluloid windmill
At the stuffed finch fastened to a hat
And at giant legs trousered in twill,
Shod in oppressor's brogues, I disowned
Their covenants and allegiances.

Let me stand outside the Wall of Death
Where the blonde woman in riding breeches
Straddles and revs up her scarlet bike.
(From her companion, the lean-jawed man
With a cowlick, I avert my thoughts.)

Later, from within, the roar of engines
Rises to frenzy and the hooped timber
Cylinder shudders under the rite—
Hidden from me where I hang around,
Learning, as always, only from hearsay.

from THE BRAY HOUSE

Eilis Ní Dhuibhne

In Eilis Ní Dhuibhne's futuristic novel, Ireland has been devastated by a nuclear disaster. A Swedish expedition discovers some survivors in a house in Bray. The following passage describes an adventure of two group members further south in the county, their travels 'south...and west and south again' mirroring those of Synge in his poem 'Prelude'.

'And where did Karl and Jenny actually go?' I prodded gently.
'Over hill and over dale.'
She's said that already.
'Towards the mountain that is known as the Sugar Loaf. That is a fine mountain, and it's easy to pick out from all the others, because of its special shape. So they walked towards that, thinking of it as a landmark, and then they walked past it, and deep, deep into the forest.'
'Forest?'
'I speak metaphorically. South they went and west and south again. Down in the direction of Ashford, Wicklow and the Sally Gap. The garden of Ireland, it is known as. They walked for two or three days, and then, in a flat field in the middle of nowhere, they saw a hill.'
'Astonishing!'
'Yes, absolutely. Because this was not a great mountain, like the Sugar Loaf, but a small, perfectly circular mound. It was covered with grey dust, as everything was in this land, but there was one narrow gap in the dust, just a few inches wide. And in that gap was a piece of grey rock.'
'Hm.'
'When Karl and Jenny arrived at this mound, Jenny had a strange sensation: the picture she carried in her mind, which was always there, night and day, changed. It began to glow. She tried to suppress it, because it glowed too brightly, it hurt her mind as a brilliant light hurts the eyes. But it would not be quenched, the more she tried to turn it out the brighter it shone. It was like a vision, but an internal one.'
'Like all vision,' I said.
'Perhaps. Jenny knew what it was: a sign from God. "We have arrived at a good place," she said to Karl.'

'And what did Karl say?'

'He was sceptical.'

He smoked his pipe, increasing the tempo slightly, so that rings of blue smoke rose in rapid succession above his head. His hair had grown, like Jenny's, and he had tied it back behind the nape of his neck in a pony tail. It looked rather silly, I thought.

'Nevertheless, they stayed close to the rock, because they arrived there just as a thick fog was sweeping across the countryside. It was so thick that it became impossible to see anything, so Karl and Jenny sat down, in the shadow of the mound, and waited for it to lift. Time passed, however, and it seemed to get worse, not better, and finally night fell.

"We will sleep here in this good place," Jenny said. 'It's safe here.' Karl was worried about the danger of sleeping in the open, but they had no choice. And since they were very tired, they fell fast asleep.'

Jenny paused and smiled distantly.

'I woke up first. The sky was clear, and I could see that the fog had lifted. There was an almost full moon, and it was very bright: the landscape looked like a moonscape, the way it does, sometimes, here. I got up carefully, so as not to waken Karl, and walked all around the mound. Really, it was exactly the same all around, but it had such a regular shape, it was shaped like an igloo, that I knew it must have been built by human hands. So... another house, I thought. So what, the country seems to be full of them. It took me about ten minutes to get right around the hillock, and when I came back to where Karl was sleeping still, I got the terrible shock: the rock we had noticed before had parted slightly, and a light was shining through the crack!'

Karen and I gasped.

'I was frightened, suddenly: I knew it must portend something good, I knew that. But it was so abrupt, and so unexpected, that I felt more scared than I have ever been in my whole life. I shook Karl violently and woke him up. He was shocked, too, but less so than I was, maybe just because I had seen the light first.'

"What shall we do?" I asked, clinging to him.

"Well, I guess we should investigate it," was what he said. But he continued to sit still, staring, and we both stayed rigid for ages, it seemed. Afraid, really, to move.

And then, the rocks parted, slowly, before our eyes. And Elinor emerged.'

'Elinor?'

'Elinor MacHugh. That is what we call her. I'll come to that in a minute. She looked—well, you've seen her. But she looked even worse then, she looked totally inhuman, I fully believed she was a ghost, or some kind of otherworld creature, the kind of thing you read about inhabiting fairy mounds in Ireland.'

FROM SUNRISE WITH SEA MONSTER

Neil Jordan

Then, on the day after De Valera presented his condolences to the German embassy on the death of Hitler, I resurrected my father.

He had died in that other sea, to the west, and this smaller one outside my window, that I fished when the light was good seemed to hold his spirit in a more companionable form. Rose was by now a memory, a bitter-sweet one, that scent of dried flowers matching the printed flowers on her dress, her upright back by the upright piano, her long blonde hair shifting as she played. I drank too much most nights, whiskey in the empty study and, when the night was clear and the humour took me, Guinness in the waterfront bars down near the Head. I would wake with the first light, walk out behind the house to where the Dargle river spilt into the harbour.

That river was a small insignificant one, almost an afterthought to the layers of sand and silt that clogged its banks, but in the early morning when it reflected the sky it had a certain muddy poetry to it. I had clear memories of a kingfisher, scudding across the brown surface with its flash of royal blue, of the mullet that would hang beneath the bridge where the sewer pipe came out. I would sit beneath the huge metal girders of the railway bridge, watch these mullet and think of how the fish we had always caught together were of the unprepossessing kind: mullet, plaice, sole, an eel or two, the lazy kind, addicted to the grosser forms of waste, fun for catching, maybe, but not eating. I would watch the somnolent arcs these mullet made, then hear the six-thirty from Cork to Dublin whacking by, shaking the earth I sat on, the huge metal girders, adding a ghostly ripple to the swatches of water, sending the mullet off in whiplike flashes to the darker corners that fish go to whenever they go.

FOUR POEMS

Caitríona O'Reilly

A Weekend in Bodega Bay

Tippi in a pea-green suit and pin-heels.
That sprawling feline smile she wears
ought to be thrown behind bars.
Crows are massing on the jungle jim.
There is the laughter of billions of birds.

Soon the sky is a limited place
full of cries and unbreathable feathers.
It is the watchful malice of women
that maddens them. Tippi
(in heels and a pea-green suit),

watches mother in her kingdom of ruined beauty.
She is driven indoors by the birds
who will eat the palms of her hands.
They leave an awful silence when they go,
a landscape of recumbent, bitten blondes.

Evening, Bray Harbour

Nothing escapes the slow, unshuttered eye
scanning the river where the rushes snag
the flashing minnow-shoals under the bridge.
The watching cormorant stands and never moves.

MICHELANGELO, THE CROUCHING BOY

They hold such broken attitudes
that once were strong enough to hold
their own in gleaming city-states:
now the marble flows in them
like burst mercury, making them fragments
of a dance to ring the room;
damaged patriarchs and footloose caryatids.

Only a waist-high boy, the centrepiece,
gives nothing of himself away.
His shoulders, knees and uncreated hands
compose a vessel of shadows, from which
he'll grow to be himself again
and so endure, if never quite become:
stone boy contemplating stone.

PERDITA

I cannot feel found.
I filled your absence in me
with all the wrong things, father,
fardels, odd bits, gewgaws,
waves in tendrils and trees like lobster-claws
and howling. Being chased.
There's a mesh of dark inside my head,
behind the face
purely my mother's—
like air shelled in light, a purple bubble,
the thin skin over a scream.

THE SWANS AT BRAY

James McNeice

Dark harbour waters brightened by a host of swans,
Did some tranquil river god gift us these quiet lives?
No storms of trading ships diminish their grace,
Only fretful men at play in sailing boats;
They know not Lir's sad children,
And wait not the calling of bells,
Faithful always, two by two, the swans glide on,
While we watch and wonder.

FROM THE NEIGHBOURHOOD OF DUBLIN

Weston St John Joyce

At this period there were only two habitations along the sea front—one a small pretty cottage where Bray Head Hotel now stands, whilst somewhere on the ground occupied by Claddagh Terrace was the other, a mud hovel, so diminutive, so wretched and so miserable as to earn for it the local soubriquet of 'The Rat Hole'. This strange dwelling was tenanted by an equally strange occupant—an eccentric, solitary, tar-begrimed old fisherman, who was a well-known character in the neighbourhood, and who took a delight in surrounding his unattractive abode with ill-smelling heaps of manure, offal, seaweed and every other abomination that came within his reach, until at last it became difficult to distinguish between the dwelling and these strange accessories. To what end he accumulated these malodorous tumuli none who knew him could surmise; but that he enjoyed the possession of them could be open to no doubt, as he was to be seen there daily, during his leisure hours, regaling his nose and eyes on their perfume and proportions.

In the other cottage near the Head lived an elderly woman and her daughter, whose ostensible means of livelihood were seeking and selling the pebbles peculiar to the locality, known as Wicklow pebbles, but who really were engaged in the profitable business of smuggling, and, in conjunction with others, acted as agents for the various overseas craft that then frequented this coast for the contraband trade.

The mother was a woman of great courage and strength of character, and always went about armed; she was known to have amassed a considerable fortune by her operations, and was, at least on one occasion, engaged in an affray with the Preventive men. When she died many years afterwards, her daughter found herself a rich woman.

The wild and lonely coast of Wicklow offered so many facilities for smuggling that the efforts of the Government were unable to accomplish more than barely to interrupt and at most delay the well-laid schemes of the contrabands.

The usual plan adopted by smuggling vessels plying here was, under cover of night or misty weather, to send their contraband goods ashore in boats to the preconcerted places of concealment on the coasts, and then to sail openly with their legitimate cargo to Dublin or other port, and thus hoodwink the Revenue authorities. There can be little doubt, however, that corruption was rife among the Revenue and Customs officers at that period, and that they could, when necessary, look in the wrong direction.

The natural conformation of the coast around Bray Head lent itself readily to the adaptation of places of concealment, of which there were several, but the principal one was that known as 'The Brandy Hole', half a mile along the shore from where the road crosses the railway on the Head. Here was an immense cavern, with its entrance opening to the sea, and its many ramifications extending far in under the hill, affording ample accommodation for the cargoes of all the vessels plying their risky trade here. Into this great natural storehouse, fully laden boats were easily able to make their way by the light of lanterns, and discharge their contents high and dry into the numerous receptacles prepared for them.

Immediately over this cavern, and adjoining the rude goat track that then encircled the Head, was a shaft sunk in a slanting direction into the earth, communicating with another subterraneous chamber—a sort of second storey to the lower one—but showing no trace of its existence on the surface, as the entrance was carefully concealed by a thick growth of brambles and bracken. This provided for the initiated a ready means of access from the land to the cavern, which was furnished where necessary with steps and platforms whereby a person above could, by means of a rope, assist those below to climb out on top, or if need be, drag up bales of goods for storage in the upper chamber.

In after years, when reports began to be whispered abroad as to the existence of this Ali Baba's cave, the locality became the scene of some fierce struggles between the Revenue men and the desperadoes engaged in the contraband traffic. It was a time when a Revenue officer's life was one of constant excitement, he needed to be a man of courage and determination, and the risks of his avocation were almost as great as those of a soldier's in the field.

SEE EMILY PLAY

Shane Harrison

I stand on the headland looking down at the town below, the sea is away to my left and the harbour ahead and to my right. The sun is sinking, swollen, into the hills and the gulls wheel and cry about the cliffs beneath me. That's the complete picture, I can put in the details later. Picture is appropriate, that is the way I see things, through a lens framed by a rectangle. The camera whirrs as I take another, and another, and another, swivelling slowly until I have it all in three hundred and sixty degrees. Are all photographs true? Does the camera ever lie? It is a question of timing, I believe, or time, you only last so long in a photograph, you really need to be there.

The last stop on my panorama is the camp site, the posh end where the big mobile homes rest. Is there anything more desolate, more heartbreaking than a caravan park at dusk, the night before the holiday season? Anything more pregnant with promise?

The night before the holiday season I would usually sit alone in my caravan, shuffling photographs of my past. I would take a bottle of wine onto the patio and drink till the sun went down. Then I would drink some more. This time I was going to stay and see it. This time I wasn't going to rent the thing out.

Each year is always going to be different. We all tell ourselves that. That's why I was staying on this year, usually I only used the place in June and September, I rented it on holiday weekends and throughout July and August. Something made me stay, I could smell life starting up again. I hoped I was right.

I suppose it was going to be different for Emily too. I had seen the kid before, pleasantly fair, supple, a good kid you would think from watching her, they were mostly good kids. It really did turn out different for Emily, for us all.

A small town nestles in the cove. There are several pubs of varying quality, a half dozen eateries mostly of the fish and chip variety, a battered cinema, two smallish supermarkets and amongst the few B&B's, one good hotel. On each end of the cove are rival amusement arcades, and on waste ground near the harbour there is a carnival at high season.

There is much more to the town than the above, of course, but the above is what I wrote, more or less, in describing the town for the travel guide which I sell some work to. They use one of the photographs I have taken also, a not very flattering one. I wonder do my efforts keep the foreign tourists away. Probably not. There are more each year and the town is losing some of that neglected quality which I love so well, so selfishly well. A couple of years ago they were saying that the town was dying, the old Grand Hotel had closed and the picturesque Marine Hotel burned down, suspiciously. People's habits had changed, they wanted sun and sex, and they got little of it here, little of the sun anyway. They were wrong, of course, but they will be right someday, inevitably they will be right about forthcoming death.

I have known them for years, the locals, and they have known me, there are even some with whom I am on first name terms, but only a few. They don't know what I do, no, they don't know they have a spy in their midst. They see me with my prying eye and they don't even guess, they haven't a clue, not a dickeybird.

In the morning, the first morning of my summer holidays—hah, that's a good one! In the morning I manage to open one eye, my squinting eye, and note that the weather is reassuringly normal. A dull grey fog envelops everything and anything more than twenty feet away is well nigh invisible. I get dressed, have a smoke and make for the town. I know where it is.

It is a twenty minute walk if I take the laneway through the fields, joining the main road into town right beside the one good hotel. Along the laneway I hear sheep bleating and scattering mingled with a naggingly familiar sound, a rasping, tingling sound. A human voice shouts and fades into the distance. But there are no stories for me in a mist, I need clear air.

I stop in the first coffee shop in the town, the Coffee Deck, such a habit of mine that I am well known there. Rachel, with her lovely green eyes and plump innocent face, greets me by name. More lovely each year, I think, less plump and less innocent too.

'So, how have you been keeping?' she begins, and we settle into familiar conversations, update ourselves on the activities of names we know. I tell her about my disintegrating family, I tell her my problems.

'Maybe things will work out.' she says, 'and you might see things much clearer, down here, away from it all.'

I point out that the mist has, so far, stopped me from seeing anything at all.

'When it lifts, then.' she says, and I realise that it was never what Rachel said that mattered so much as the way she said it. It is that beautiful musical lilt that seems to squash all pessimism. When it lifts, then, and I repeat that phrase in my own flat monotone:

'When it lifts.'

I am distracted as I see Emily and some friends ghost past the window, I feel a sudden, strange, lurch in my stomach and am torn, inexplicably, between a desire for her to come in and some unnamed dread that she will do so. Rachel, who has been talking about photography, is suddenly snapping her fingers before my eyes.

'Oy! Anyone home?'

She follows my eyes and grimaces, not seeing anything there, everything swallowed by the mist. I apologise and listen again to her news and her plans. I should pay closer attention to such things, if not for a friend then for myself, after all, I could use the money.

There is a cannon pointing out to sea. That is a little joke; there are two, I am sitting on the cannon and pointing my Canon out to sea. 'Bejesus, it's Cher shooting a new video.' I turn to see my favourite culchie advancing towards me off the dock. Sean Dwyer, local auctioneer, his hands in his pockets and the flap of his blazer fluttering behind him. Sean really does have a red neck, and even though he is a former inter-county footballer and built like a prop-forward, I can get away with ribbing him about it.

I get some work off Sean, not a lot, dribs and drabs, but it's work and we'll usually seal the deal with a mother of all drinking bouts. We get on.

'Fucking Jackeens. Won't believe it unless you photograph it.'

'I thought that was Yanks.' I point the camera at him to annoy him.

'Please! Unless you want to deliver it later at St Mary's.' St. Mary's being the local maternity hospital.

We chew the fat, he knows my situation and skirts around it; his wife, Jean, and mine are friends. It all goes way back. He's planning an expedition—out to the islands, a spot of fishing—and asks me to come along.

'You'll love it. And if you start going on about art we can maroon you on Seal Island!'

'What, again?' This is true, they did that once although I think it was a genuine error—they simply forgot that I had been with them. I accept.

'You just behave.' says Sean and smiles. He changes tack abruptly, 'Have you seen my gobshite son?'

'Brian?' Sean has two boys and Colm, the eldest, has just started university.

'Ay, Brian.' says Sean, and with a resigned, vaguely defeated shrug, turns and walks briskly away. 'If you see him, send him home.' he shouts over his shoulder, and is gone. I wonder about Brian for a moment, some people make you wonder.

Last year was our last family holiday, last year we all played happy families here at the beach. The White Strand, treacherous at full tide with the river flowing in to the south, is best at low tide with its wide expanse of beach uncovered and the rock pools below the cliffs facing north. On the second day I am there already, reliving it all. I see Sile walk the kids, Lena and Barry, towards the pounding surf, I feel the sun on my skin, I turn another page of the book. There is somebody watching me.

There is nobody watching me now. There are few here, around the corner of the cliffs is the cove where the people go to watch the dolphin play. Here, today, on the second day, there is a couple up on the rocks, sunning themselves in the faint sun. She is stripped to the waist and he, long-haired and fat, is naked. It is distracting, they are so oblivious of everything and I am so aware of them. They weren't there last year, you didn't do that sort of thing last year; but there is no point thinking about that— I know that I cannot go back there.

Someone is watching me. I remember turning that page and...two girls are walking the sandy path down from the fields. Mid teens in one piece swimsuits, one carries a shortened surf board. It is Emily, and she floats past without even a sideways glance.

When Lena and Barry returned, breathless, they were full of garbled excitement about the surf board.

'Lady let us use her surfboard,' Barry gasped.

Lena was older and not so easily impressed; 'She was no lady,' she scoffed.

Sile and I had a good laugh at that, much to Lena's disgust. 'I meant she was only a *girl*' she insisted. I think it's what I miss most, really, the laughing at nothing, the private jokes. Oh, I miss the warmth at night, I do, I miss that too.

The sun comes out on the second day. My hangover is not nearly so bad, although there is a curious taste in my mouth. I hear the shouts and the sheep, again—what is going on out there? There are holes in my memory. I remember it took me ages getting to sleep, the bigger kids were playing for ever in the playground, for ever and ever. I hope I hadn't done anything foolish, like telling them to fuck off, but there is a vague and immature recollection of giggling and footsteps in the dark. What of it!

At the Coffee Deck Rachel asks me to the dance. Just like that. She's talking to a couple of local youths and she shouts over to me: 'Oy, Neil, are you coming to the dance on Saturday?'

Me? I was miles away and a bit embarrassed to see the three white faces turn to me. I hummed and hawed.

'Ah, forget it,' she said. The boys smirked.

One of the boys was Brian, Sean's son. I remember then that he had been hanging around the playground at the site. I remembered his voice and I remembered the name he called. That was the name and the laughter that echoed through my sleep.

I am of that age where I begin to consider the merit of such clichés that youth is wasted on the young—I suppose so much of it was wasted on me. Wrapped in such gloomy thoughts I have a solitary pint at Moriarty's and walk back towards the site. Rachel hails me from the coffee Deck. She's all business now, talking about the photographs I had apparently agreed to do for the refurbishment.

The refurbishment? Rachel is taking over the Deck, as it will be called, she is, she says, going to be a mover and a shaker. I can well believe it. The earlier business seems forgotten until I turn to leave.

'You know your problem?' she says, 'You think you're too old, but you've never really grown up.'

'Eh?'

'The dance. You're afraid to go in case people look at you and say: ah, the oldest swinger in town.'

'I'm not afraid...'

'You're afraid, like a boy would be afraid. You've got to take your place in the world...'

'Act like a man?'

'Just be yourself.'

'Jesus, I'll go to the bloody dance if you want...'

'You don't have to go if you don't want to.'

'I'll go!'

With that Rachel was suddenly satisfied and set about her dusting and polishing, the mid-day sun having burned off the customers. I left, red-faced, unsure whether that constituted a date or a challenge. What an odd woman, I thought, what a strange *girl*.

That evening I take my glass of wine, I take my beaker of wine, over to the perimeter fence where there is a good view of the sea and the lights of the town below. Up to my left the green sward is glowing, melting down over the cliffs. The folly on top looks majestic, dramatic against the cerulean sky. I consider strolling up there and taking a time exposure.

So I find myself as evening falls climbing along the green edge of the cliffs towards the ancient folly. Gulls are wheeling and away to the right, where I dare to peep over the precipice I see they have white streaked the cliffs around their cacophonous city. I have to lie on my belly to look over the edge and as I do the roll I have taken today slips from my breast pocket and slithers over the side. It bounces down the steep slope towards the very edge where it lodges on a stone. Well, fuck it anyway. A brave man would go and retrieve his property, it had taken me all day to get those shots, aye, a foolish man would risk his life for a day's work. I could take them again. So the light would be different and the details would never be the same, but the details never are. Worse and worse again was the fact that I had sneaked some pictures of Emily. Sneak is not really the word; herself and Brian were hanging around together down at the boardwalk, near the dolphin trips, and I went and asked them, actually asked them, would they mind. They didn't, in fact they were naturals, as young lovers are; at least Emily, tanned and Titian-haired, seemed a natural to me. So sneak isn't the word. Fuck it anyway.

Again I hear the sheep and the shouts, and the harsh rasp of something metallic. Distracted, a bit irritated, I turn onto my side to look up towards where the noise is coming from. I see the sheep scattering over the hillside and behind them, cutting through them now, a stiff figure on a bike, whooping and ringing his raspy bell. There is something amusing about the scene and my curiosity draws me towards it. I forget about the film and head towards the ditch. The man on the bike has reached the bottom of the field and turns around to push his bike up the hill again. I walk parallel to him and hail him at the top.

He looks a sprightly fifty something, a shock of iron grey hair and creased features giving him a passing resemblance to Samuel Beckett. I had taken him to be a local, since the place is flush with eccentrics, but his accent is foreign, Australian or maybe South African. There is something about his wild eyes that convey a sense of religious fervour. I tell him he could herd better with a dog.

He laughs. 'I'm not herding, I'm chasing.'

'Why chase sheep?'

He shrugs, 'Because they're there.' It's my turn to laugh. We exchange cigarettes and chat easily for a while. He has been living here for almost a year, an oasis of sanity in a mad, mad world is his explanation. There is a past buried in there, something he's not going to tell me so I don't ask.

'I see you take photographs,' he says.

'Don't all tourists?'

'Are you a tourist?' It wasn't really a question and I can only shrug, non-commitedly, in reply. He hoists up his bike again, with mock weariness, and returns to his sport. 'I think they quite like it really,' he says, and heads off down the hill again.

I call into Sean the next day to see if he has any small premises to let. If I'm going to stay here for the summer I will need a decent darkroom, hell, even an indecent darkroom. Sean is more interested in the fishing expedition.

'Can you bestir yourself tomorrow and pick us up some bait, the other lads are busy and I'm...'

I am prepared for this and have a litany of cast iron excuses prepared.

'Y'know,' says Sean, 'You'd be better off going down to the chipper and getting a battered cod and chips. And you can puke up after it instead of before it as you'll be doing tomorrow, because you're fuck all use in a boat.'

I was telling him about the roll of film when Brian dropped in. He had Emily in tow, and she stood sullen guard by the door. I gave her the most imperceptible of nods and she replied in kind. If she was following this lanky streak of misery who was now panning for his father's gold then she did it with a suitable air of diffidence; yet I had sensed in Emily over the last few days that sense of desperation, that over eager flaunting of herself that spoke as much of needs and wants as it did of desire.

'Ah, you gobshite,' Sean said as he turned to his son, then laughed when he saw Brian's face drop. 'I'm talking to him, to Neil. Dropped his roll of film over the cliff at the folly. Stuck there, just above the drop. Bejesus, just as well it wasn't a wedding roll, you'd be winching it up by helicopter.'

'I'll get them for you, if you like,' Brian said, he had a surprisingly meek voice for his loutish appearance.

'You, mister,' said Sean, 'Can keep away from those cliffs, if I hear...'

Brian switched on his look of teenage disdain and Sean relented, shoving a note at him, 'Here's a fecking tenner, now don't spend it on anything that smells.'

My eyes were drawn reluctantly back to Emily. She was staring at me with deep ambiguity. If you want it, that look seemed to say, get it yourself. Whatever it is, get it yourself.

I wasn't the oldest at the dance, not by a long chalk. Sean was there holding up the bar. Apparently it was the best known late extension in the county, the things you miss when you have young kids! So, for the first time in eight years visiting the town I put my elbow into a pool of beer and ordered a pint without even thinking of losing my glass slipper in the rush home.

'Where the fuck were you, today?'

'I didn't think you needed me.'

'Jesus, you're terrible fucking sensitive all the same.'

I asked them did they catch anything at about the same time that the band started up again and I caught precious little of the subsequent yarn, nothing but the odd spray of spittle, several expletives and a few references to his 'gobshite son' who apparently was filling my spot in the boat. By the end of the tale I was scanning the perimeter of the floor for signs of...I wasn't too sure, actually, who.

Rachel rescued me later, stealing up behind me and poking me in the ribs. She was radiant or maybe drunk, probably both, and was trailing a rat-faced youth, swigging from a bottle, who seemed about to go for my throat each time he spoke. Rachel, after an age of screaming in my ear, eventually got me onto the dance floor and we left the rat in the increasingly maudlin company of Sean. I see his drowning eyes follow me onto the floor but I don't dwell on that. As I fold into Rachel's embrace I think how pleasantly she cushions our collision and yet, yet how small and fragile are her shoulders, her back. I am enjoying myself at last. I married too young, I really did, and surrendered too soon to the unique solitude of responsibility. Oh, all the things I had been missing.

We float past the bar again and I see Sean's eyes unglaze and look towards me with sudden precision. But it is not at me that he is looking, we have bumped against Brian and Emily, and I see Brian's eyes looking defiantly back at his father, and I see Emily's eyes cast upwards in adoration, but not quite adoration.

The dance ends and we spill out into the garish light of the carpark. Suddenly it occurs to me that I have no place to go, there is no place like home and there is no place to go. I look at Rachel and see how much she belongs here, as much a part of the town as the mountains and the harbour and the amusements; the tides that have washed over her and retreated back to sea, the comings and goings of the dolphin; she might come and go herself - but this will always be her place.

There is a chip van where we dally before giving up, we are stuck for a while with the rat-faced youth and his catch of the night in a round of joke telling and cigarette swapping that passes off well enough before finding ourselves alone. Alone on the high road leading up towards the site.

It gets to the point that Rachel is standing closer than she should and for a giddy moment, no, longer than that really, I feel that I should fuck her, that the two of us should fuck like minks somewhere in the feral undergrowth. And I feel, in so much as I can ever be confident in predicting such things, that the chances of it coming to pass is in fact better than fifty-fifty, is closer to ninety or ninety five per cent. So, I could find myself in a field, or in a stony cove, heavily exploring those parts of Rachel about which I previously have idly speculated, and that I would screw her rigid not once but several times before the cock crowed. And then, and then...?

When it all came to pass, it never happened at all. We watched the moon evaporate above the deepest and calmest of seas, finished off the sixpack, cracking open the tops with her sharp teeth, smoking ourselves to ecstatic and isolated death. Tomorrow, we said when we parted, tomorrow.

There are two paths back to the site, the high road as I have mentioned, and a low path, a dirt track that skirts the bay and is favoured by fishermen, and young lovers.

On the high road there is a particularly scenic vantage point overlooking the bay, the town below and the mountainous far shore. Tonight under a full moon, with the moonlight and streetlight flickering in unison in the dewy early Summer air, it is achingly beautiful. I lean on the wall there and smoke my last cigarette. My eyes are focussed on the low path. Just there where it bends around the rocks a couple embrace, oblivious to the fact that they are highlighted by the one streetlamp on that dark stretch of road. Perhaps oblivious. It is Emily and Brian. What are they doing? What is she going to do for him? I wonder if, looking out at the world over his shoulder, if she can see the match flare in my cupped hands and cast a menacing shadow across my face.

In that uneasy sleep my dreams are haunted by ghosts, my body struggles against drowning in the storm-tossed sheets. I am so alone out here, so desperately alone, yet when dawn steals in to take another night from me I sense a figure cold and impassive, loom above the bed. Blearily I look up towards the misty face and it leans down to me. It is the face of some poor wretch, a beggar or a thief, the expression frozen in a mirthless gurn that it has fooled itself into believing is a smile. But there is something awful that I recognise in there, those thin lips and hooded eyes, the hot, supercilious stare; I see my father dying and I close my eyes again. I feel its breath on my cheek, the stench of old alcohol and spicy meat, the voice is nasal and rasping, oh, I have heard that voice before.

'You are afraid,' it says.

'Of what?' I ask, 'Of death?'

'No, not death. Death is easy. You get used to death and there is so little to do.'

'Who are you?' I ask, getting colder and colder.

'I am the reason you are afraid.' it says, the voice mercifully getting weaker, pulling the cold off somewhere with it, 'I am you. Yes, if you opened your eyes you'd see, I am you.'

A drunken cackle echoes around the van and as it grows fainter I manage to sneak my eyes open, but there is nothing there. I chew on the vile gum of sleep, parched and empty, if only I could have tasted Rachel's kisses or captured the merest hint of her perfume. But there is nothing there, and no place to go—but home.

One last time I mount the hill towards the folly, so apt that, so apt; and from that vantage point the town will be so small that I can hold it in the palm of my hand. What more disasters can I prevail upon its inhabitants, what more love can I lavish on them, or on some of them, never to have it understood, never to have it truly requited. It is said that amongst primitive peoples there is a great suspicion, a superstition regarding photography; they are convinced that the photograph captures more than the image and that it captures the soul as well. They know this not through knowledge of the process but through intuition; how wise they are to put their trust in that!

I climb the hill one last time and hear the bleating of the sheep and shouts, the music of the spokes and rasping bells. Over to my right a slight figure is perched precariously on the cliff's edge and I notice flowers have been strewn underfoot, but I cannot linger now. I reach the top of the hill in time to see the man, the priest, I suppose, complete his first run and turn to push his bike up to the summit again.

I rise to meet him when he comes close, but while he is friendly, happy even, I have noticed something weary in his step.

'A fine day,' I say.

'Ay, thanks be to God,' he answers, with a practised local nuance. He turns those steel blue eyes out to sea.

The dolphin is jumping in the bay, boy is that dolphin up for it. 'It's well for some.' I say.

He thinks a moment with his face still turned from me. You've seen that profile before, from out of the darkness as the hatch slides back, it knows your secrets, or thinks it does.

'They say that the dolphin has found a lover,' he says, 'and that he is going to follow her out to sea.'

'The town will miss him, he'll take a lot of the trade with him.'

The priest thinks a moment and turns to look into my eyes; 'But he will be back amongst his own.'

Our eyes turn now to the figure on the cliff, I recognise her and remark how dangerous it is there, just as Sile would have, had she been here. 'A wind could come and...'

'But it has. Haven't you heard?'

I make my way back towards the site in some confusion. I come to where Emily waits at the spot where I had dropped my roll on Friday. She walks towards me without any apparent recognition, she clutches a homemade wooden cross to her chest.

'A boy died here last night,' she says. 'But I can't get this cross into the ground.'

She holds out a crumpled piece of paper to me, it has been torn from a newspaper and is part of a photograph of a schoolboy football team hoisting the cup of victory. I know that photograph, it hangs on the wall of Sean Dwyer's office.

'This is the boy?'

She nods; 'It's the only photograph I have.' She looks back towards the cliff edge and passes the cross, almost offhandedly, to me. Emily has made some attempt to point the butt of the cross but the ground is hard and it doesn't penetrate easily.

For days I could see the impression it left on my palms but at least I got it to stand in the earth, and that was what she wanted. She thanked me and I left her there, there was nothing more to do.

I did not go to the funeral. Nothing remained. The next morning, very early, I packed up and left, drove out along the only road and kept on driving as it widened and widened, I was taking the river home from its source unto the sea. I never looked back, I never went back, I only went home.

Some years later I saw the ex-priest on television. I was right, he had been a priest. He talked about faith and redemption. He talked about his experiences in the town. He even talked about God. He told us that the dolphin had found a mate, the dolphin had found a mate and had wandered back to sea. All things come to an end, all things come to pass. I don't really think about it all that often.

TWO POEMS

Jerome O'Loughlin

Number 15 Usher's Island

A biting wind from the mouth of the Liffey,
As I stroll past Number 15 Usher's Island,
Boarded up now, a preservation order on it,
And see Gabriel and Gretta Conroy in my mind's eye,
Arrive by cab from Monkstown in the lightly falling snow,
To attend his Aunt Kate and Aunt Julia Morkan's annual Xmas dance—
Miss Kate is a music teacher, Miss Julia leading soprano in Adam and
    Eve's—
Gretta climbing the steps to the Georgian door, her blue felt hat,
Bronze-coloured hair, and her black cloak, flecked with snow,
Her husband paying the cabman and giving a florin over the fare,
A light fringe of snow lying like a cape on the shoulders of his frieze
    overcoat,
Like toecaps on the toes of his galoshes.

You Had No Bone to Pick, Sam Beckett, with Graveyards

You had no bone to pick, Sam Beckett, with graveyards.
Hands clasped behind your back, you often wandered
Among headstones, noting the inscriptions, in Glasnevin,
In the ancient graveyard at Tully, here in Redford,
A small seaside cemetery, where your parents rest,
Their names now blurred on the Wicklow granite headstone,
Purple heather, once contained, now smothering their grave.
You picnicked here too, relishing with a flask of tea,
Sandwiches, slices of fruit cake, biscuits,
Tasting sweeter when you were sitting on a tomb.

THE OPPRESSION OF THE HILLS

John Millington Synge

Among the cottages that are scattered through the hills of County Wicklow I have met with many people who show in a singular way the influence of a particular locality. These people live for the most part beside old roads and pathways where hardly one man passes in the day, and look out all the year on unbroken barriers of heath. At every season heavy rains fall for often a week at a time, till the thatch drips with water stained to a dull chestnut, and the floor in the cottages seems to be going back to the condition of the bogs near it. Then the clouds break, and there is a night of terrific storm from the south-west—all the larches that survive in these places are bowed and twisted towards the point where the sun rises in June—when the winds come down through the narrow glens with the congested whirl and roar of a torrent, breaking at times for sudden moments of silence that keep up the tension of the mind. At such times the people crouch all night over a sod of turf and the dogs howl in the lanes.

When the sun rises there is a morning of almost supernatural radiance, and even the oldest men and women come out into the air with the joy of children who have recovered from a fever. In the evening it is raining again. This peculiar climate, acting on a population that is already lonely and dwindling, has caused or increased a tendency to nervous depression among the people, and every degree of sadness, from that of the man who is merely mournful to that of the man who has spent half his life in the madhouse, is common among these hills.

Not long ago in a desolate glen in the south of the county I met two policemen driving an ass-cart with a coffin on it, and a little further on I stopped an old man and asked him what had happened.

'This night three weeks,' he said, 'there was a poor fellow below reaping in the glen, and in the evening he had two glasses of whiskey with some other lads. Then some excitement took him, and he threw off his clothes and ran away into the hills. There was great rain that night, and I suppose the poor creature lost his way, and was the whole night perishing in the dark and darkness. In the morning they found his naked footmarks on some mud half a mile above the road, and again where you go up by a big stone. Then there was nothing known of him till last night, when they found his body on the mountain, and it near eaten by the crows.'

Then he went on to tell me how different the country had been when he was a young man.

'We had nothing to eat at that time,' he said, 'but milk and stirabout and potatoes, and there was a fine constitution you wouldn't meet this day at all. I remember when you'd see forty boys and girls below there on a Sunday evening, playing ball and diverting themselves; but now all this country is gone lonesome and bewildered, and there's no man knows what ails it.'

There are so few girls left in these neighbourhoods that one does not often meet with women that have grown up unmarried. I know one, however, who has lived by herself for fifteen years in a tiny hovel near a crossroads much frequented by tinkers and ordinary tramps. As she has no one belonging to her, she spends a good deal of her time wandering through the country, and I have met her in every direction, often many miles from her own glen. 'I do be so afeard of the tramps,' she said to me one evening. 'I live all alone, and what would I do at all if one them lads was to come near me? When my poor mother was dying, "Now, Nanny," says she, "don't be living on here when I am dead," says she; "it'd be too lonesome." And now I wouldn't wish to go again' my mother, and she dead—dead or alive I wouldn't go again' my mother—but I'm after doing all I can, and I can't get away by any means.' As I was moving on she heard, or thought she heard, a sound of distant thunder.

'Ah, your honour,' she said, 'do you think it's thunder we'll be having? There's nothing I fear like the thunder. My heart isn't strong—I do feel it—and I have a lightness in my head, and often when I do be excited with the thunder I do be afeard I might die there alone in the cottage and no one know it. But I do hope that the Lord—bless His holy name!—has something in store for me. I've done all I can, and I don't like going again' my mother and she dead. And now good evening, your honour, and safe home.'

Intense nervousness is common also with much younger women. I remember one night hearing someone crying out and screaming in the house where I was staying. I went downstairs and found it was a girl who had been taken in from a village a few miles away to help the servants. That afternoon her two younger sisters had come to see her, and now she had been taken with a panic that they had been drowned going home through the bogs, and she was crying and wailing, and saying she must go to look for them. It was not thought fit for her to leave the house alone so late in the evening, so I went with her. As we passed down a steep hill of heather, where the nightjars were clapping their wings in the moonlight, she told me a long story of the way she had been frightened. When we reached a solitary cottage on the edge of the bog, and as a light was still shining in the window, I knocked at the door and asked if they had seen or heard anything. When they understood our errand three half-dressed generations came out to jeer at us on the doorstep.

'Ah, Maggie,' said the old woman, 'you're a cute one. You're the girl likes a walk in the moonlight. Whist your talk of them big lumps of childer, and look at Martin Edward there, who's not six, and he can go through the bog five times in an hour and not wet his feet.'

My companion was still unconvinced, so we went on. The rushes were shining in the moonlight, and one flake of mist was lying on the river. We looked into one bog-hole, and then into another, where a snipe rose and terrified us. We listened: a cow was chewing heavily in the shadow of a bush, two dogs were barking on the side of a hill, and there was a cart far away upon the road. Our teeth began to chatter with the cold of the bog air and the loneliness of the night. I could see that the actual presence of the bog had shown my companion the absurdity of her fears, and in a little while we went home.

The older people in County Wicklow, as in the rest of Ireland, still show a curious affection for the landed classes wherever they have lived for a generation or two upon their property. I remember an old woman, who told me, with tears streaming on her face, how much more lonely the country had become since the 'quality' had gone away, and gave me a long story of how she had seen her landlord shutting up his house and leaving his property, and of the way he had died afterwards, when the 'grievance' of it broke his heart. The younger people feel differently, and when I was passing this landlord's house, not long afterwards, I found these lines written in pencil on the door-post:

> In the days of rack-renting
> And land-grabbing so vile
> A proud, heartless landlord
> Lived here a great while.
> When the League it was started,

And the land-grabbing cry,
To the cold North of Ireland
He had for to fly.

A year later the door-post had fallen to pieces, and the inscription with it.

FROM THE SHADOW OF THE GLEN

John Millington Synge

TRAMP. Is it go away and leave you, and you having a wake, lady of the house? I will not, surely. [*He takes a drink from his glass, which he has beside him.*] And it's none of your tea I'm asking either.

[*He goes on stitching. Nora makes the tea.*]

MICHAEL. [*After looking at the tramp rather scornfully for a moment.*] That's a poor coat you have, God help you, and I'm thinking it's a poor tailor you are with it.

TRAMP. If it's a poor tailor I am, I'm thinking it's a poor herd does be running backward and forward after a little handful of ewes, the way I seen yourself running this day, young fellow, and you coming from the fair.

[*Nora comes back to the table.*]

NORA. [*To Michael, in a low voice.*] Let you not mind him at all, Michael Dara; he has a drop taken, and it's soon he'll be falling asleep.

MICHAEL. It's no lie he's telling; I was destroyed, surely. They were that wilful they were running off into one man's bit of oats, and another man's bit of hay, and tumbling into the red bog till it's more like a pack of old goats than sheep they were... Mountain ewes is a queer breed, Nora Burke, and I not used to them at all.

NORA. [*Setting the tea-things.*] There's no one can drive a mountain ewe but the men do be reared in the Glenmalure, I've heard them say, and above by Rathvanna, and the Glen Imaal—men the like of Patch Darcy, God spare his soul, who would walk through five hundred sheep and miss one of them, and he not reckoning them at all.

MICHAEL. [*Uneasily.*] Is it the man went queer in his head the year that's gone?

NORA. It is, surely.

SONG

Friedhelm Rathjen

Wick high or low
I'll have to go
To where the sun-rays rise
Above the hills
Sam smiles and kills
The gods that spoil the skies

Sweat fills my arse
With life on Mars
While Venus drives me mad
The pedals ache
But hearts don't break
On Djouce and Featherbed

Forget the stars
Forgets the cars
Forget the scenic thing
Classics are dead
Romanticists head
For me: the bones of Synge

FROM ACTS OF SUBVERSION

Liz McManus

Claraville was a school that prided itself on its vocation to educate the daughters of the propertied class.

'You are privileged girls,' Reverend Mother could say without fear of contradiction. 'You will become the mothers and wives of the leaders of the country. Yours is a unique vocation; to guide your future husbands and children in the ways of Our Lord and His Holy Mother. This year, we are blessed to receive two girls who have been called to a higher vocation still. *La crème de la crème.* Our two postulants will become, God willing, brides of Christ himself. In your prayers, please remember your sisters, Mary Pankhurst and Jean Mulhall.'

Hanky-Panky and Jinno. Sloughing off their nicknames they disappeared beyond the heavy doors that protected the nuns from the insatiable curiosity of schoolgirls. No girl was permitted down that corridor but they jostled madly for a glimpse. An out-of-bounds raid brought back reports of underwear in laundry baskets. Pink bloomers! Oh delish…

> *Mother Stan was a silly old nun,*
> *Whose knickers were the colour of the sun.*
> *The knicks got mislaid.*
> *How old Stanislaus prayed.*
> *But she still ended up with none on!*

After lights out, smothered laughter persisted in the dormitory until Mother Stanislaus lifted her head from her beads and her angry *girls!* barked down along the cubicles.

RETURNING TO KILCOOLE

Aidan Mathews

Hubcaps, horsedroppings rubble the sand.
Although I had managed to remember
The fabulous frenzy of alarmed snipe,
Hedges brown as a smoker's fingers,
The railway track was foremost in my mind.

Often in my eagerness, I anklesprained
Among those rails, was always terrified
Of trains running me over, had nightmares
Full of broken skulls, revolving wheels.
I used go there with my godfather
Who had a blackthorn and noticed everything.

I grew up to his hip, elbow, shoulder:
Then it was time to begin remembering
Important things. The heron we both saw
through his binoculars when I was twelve
And informed him it was a flamingo;
Or the time we were there around midnight

To hear the ocean perspiring and blacker
Than tar. I suppose I was about fourteen
And needed to be alone and so we put
Two hundred yards between the two of us.
I think we were closer then than ever before.

FOUR POEMS

Bill Tinley

FROM STRONGHOLDS

THREECASTLES

The afternoon has turned to rain
As we pull our bikes up slowly,
Hauling them over the low fence.
We push quickly through the damp grass
And lean the shining frames against
The dry gable of the stone wall.

The noise of a car on the road
Pins us breathless on our hunkers
Until it passes. Then we rise
And slip headfirst, one at a time,
Into the cold, mud-floored dungeon,
Straightening our backs to look up.

A leg up and I grip the ledge
And rest for a minute before
Offering you a helping hand.
Round and round we climb the staircase,
Stopping to savour each chamber,
The vertigo of broken floors.

The lichen-covered battlements
Open to the strong mountain wind,
Reveal the unbordered terrain
Around this abandoned outpost—
State forestry, manured farmland,
The steel-grey waters of the lake.

Golden Hill

A shadow dash across the hillside
Streaks the bracken and the batch of trees,
A soft wind ruffles the new meadow
To a wave of sea-green at our knees.
The crude dam we built one spring afternoon
Is now a monument to childhood;
The moss-grown stones, and cold bog-water
Running like memory says it should.
Behind thick-thorned ditches of defence
Was a strange ground, not for our walking,
Where the hillside foxes hid by day
And left at night for hen-runs, stalking
In caution as we did in fear.
There's the thinned-out trail of disuse
That wormed to school just for farmers' sons;
A swinging-tree with a broken noose
And pen-knifed names of people who've changed.
There's a hoof-pocked path where hunters ride
Close to the hedge, through the balding wood
And down the undiscovered side.
Nights come alive, of lights, foolish dogs,
And half-mindedly lamping rabbits
When someone laughed and we all went home.
Or mornings marching through cuckoo spit
Because that was the time for mushrooms.
Across the mill-race, under the moon,
Up close to the stars at night we went;
The placeless owl crooned her wood-haunting tune
Down the deep valley of drains and dung.
At sunset, the hill's a silhouette
In a halo of red promises
That dash too often in tomorrow's dawn wet.
O hill of a million sundowns!
Village of fern-thatched, stone-walled cabins!
Let me bathe in your fountainous dream,
Forgive my growing up its age-old sin.

SMALL TALK

Tonight, you say, the moon looks beautiful.
Already it is halfway round the sky,
Its head in the clouds, tailing the burnt eye
It follows day and night, over the hill,
Beyond the short horizon cramped with trees,
With aerials, a solitary rook,
A terracotta curtain-lace of smoke
Hanging upside-down from neighbours' chimneys.

Such small talk we indulge in, as if moon
And sun, the stars, whatever else we praise,
Surpass the daily lives they look upon,
Conferring on us light and heat, long days
In which to wake and work, compose our hymns,
Dark nights for love and rest and pleasant dreams.

A Postcard from Teggiano
for Giovanna Cimino

A boy on tiptoe drinks fresh water there.
I sense his summertime delirium
Swallowing mouthfuls, his awkward pleasure
Balanced and braced against the fountain's rim;
A spatula of sunlight lays its tongue
On stone and step as if beseeching him
For just one splash of water. He's too young
To care about how soon the shadows stretch,
How what me might have touched falls out of reach.

These are the signs by which we might be taught
But there is dust already on your card,
I can't make out the postmark's faded date
And since you sent it, not another word
Has passed between us. What we might have known
Remains mysterious and unshared,
The thirsty boy turns round and is a man
And only hoping next time we'll know more
Sustains us in the shadows of the hour.

POULAPHOUCA RESERVOIR

Dennis O'Driscoll

'Where ivy grows on a house, the family gets worn out'
            —from the Poulaphouca Survey

1. The name 'Poulaphouca' means the hole of the spirit. Quernstones by the submerged cottages will be ground in the mills of God, fine as the distinction between Father, Son and Holy Spirit.

2. *The Shell Guide to Ireland* calls it 'the great lake of the Liffey hydro-electric works'.

3. Life goes on in that Atlantis. Ivy grows on houses. Haws redden in autumn. Roses are pruned back. Thatch is replenished. Bridal veils float like surf on the clear-skinned water. Turf fires blaze in the lake at sunset.

4. The Field at the Bottom of the Lane is at the bottom of the lake. The Field Under the Well is under water. A school of fish chases in The School House Field. The Coarse Little Field, The Field at the Back of the House, The Inside Field are flooded permanently. Garnaranny, Farnafowluch, Carnasillogue, Coolyemoon are spoken of in bubbles.

5. During summers of drought, you can see outlines of houses. Their owners' names linger at the tip of the lake's tongue. Chimneys poke above water like the blowholes of hunted whales.

FROM IRISH QUESTIONS

Michael Hamburger

for Dennis and Julie

What can they find here to feed on,
All these Irish corvidae,
The black, and the hooded crows,
The rooks, the magpies, the choughs,
Ubiquitous jackdaws, lone ravens,
With the live sheep even so sparse
On Wicklow's bare hills?
Or the sparrowhawks, where no sparrows chirped?

A great hunger it must be
For them too, though they seem to thrive
On desolation, on emptiness,
Competing with gulls on the coasts,
Competing with nothing
Above the open or covered wounds
The peat-cutters leave;
Above the alien mansions
Abandoned or burnt out,
Alien gardens and parks
Lying vacant behind closed gates
Till the bogs take over again;
Above alien barracks that guarded the landlords once
And did so still when cleared to house
The delinquent offspring of tenants;
Above the little church
Whose roof of stone resisted,
And the monks' fortress, intact,
Slate grave-slab long weathered nameless,
Cross or two still upright,
Ancient trees dropping their branches.

Black against black,
Grey against grey,
Crows glide and land
Under travelling clouds,
Now bedraggled in sudden showers,
Now glossy in sunshine,
Grey, black against green.

FROM THE WICKLOW WORLD OF ELIZABETH SMITH

Elizabeth Smith

Alas! the famine progresses; here it is in frightful reality to be seen in every face. Idle, improvident, reckless, meanly dependant on the upper classes whom they so abuse; call the bulk of the Irish what we will, and no name is too hard almost for them, here they are starving round us, cold, naked, hungry, well nigh houseless. To rouse them from their natural apathy may be the work of future years. To feed them must be our business this. Baltiboys is in comfort, few of our people in real distress, some in want of assistance and they get it, others in need of nothing. My habit of going constantly about among them keeps me pretty well acquainted with their condition, but lest I should miscalculate I am taking the whole estate regularly through at this time. Two days of visiting introduced me to no distress, only to two cases of struggling—that expressive word. I mean to make a catalogue raisonné of our population to leave among our family archives as a curiosity for future squires and a guide to us now.

Hal has killed a beef for our poor and we make daily a large pot of good soup which is served gratis to 22 people at present. It is ready at one o'clock and I thought it quite a pretty sight yesterday in the kitchen all the workmen coming in for their portion, a quart with a slice of the beef; half of them get this one day for a dinner with a bit of their own bread; the other half get milk and the cheap rice we have provided for them. Next day they reverse the order. The Colonel is giving them firing too; so they are really comfortable; there are twelve of them and ten pensioners, old feeble men and women, or those with large families of children; some of them no longer living on our ground yet once having been connected with us we can't desert them.

So far well; but beyond our small circle what a waste of misery; how are we to relieve it? Such a dense population squatted here and there upon neglected properties, dying with want, wretched every year, but ruined this. At the Relief Committee yesterday it was resolved to institute soup kitchens at proper stations for general relief, to be supported by subscription, each subscriber to have a certain number of tickets. I think the gentlemen doing this, the ladies must combine for clothing fund. The rags are scarcely coverings for decency; beds and bedding there are none, among the mob I mean; such misery crushes hope, yet hope I will. 'Hope and Wait' as was Dante's motto.

FROM BALLYKNOCKAN: A WICKLOW STONECUTTERS' VILLAGE

Séamas Ó Maitiú and Barry O'Reilly

Dónal remembers one night a strange car pulling into Brady's yard. It had come all the way from Cork and carried representatives from a committee set up to erect a memorial to Michael Collins at his birthplace, Sam's Cross. The men from Cork could not believe it when they saw a picture of Collins on the wall in Brady's house when they walked in. Brady's were great admirers of Collins and so is Dónal and he could not but join in the scheme. The committee was looking for a piece of Wicklow granite to mark the "Big Fella's" birthplace and had been directed to Ballyknockan.

The Ballyknockan people were curious as to why a more local stone was not selected as being much more convenient for the job. They were told a moving story as to why only Wicklow granite would be acceptable. When the Cork committee thought about erecting such a memorial they approached the sisters of Collins, then still alive, and asked them for their opinion on a suitable monument. They immediately replied that they would like Wicklow granite. When asked why, they went on to tell the story of Mick's last visit to his home place.

When he came home all the local people gathered into the house for a party with singing and dancing, which went on till the early hours. As people began to drift home a local man piped up and asked Mick a question: 'you have been all over Ireland, Mick; and met people from every county, which of them do you like the best?' Mick's answer was, without any hesitation 'the people from County Wicklow.' The next day, according to Dónal, he was killed at Béal na mBláth. That is why Michael's sisters wanted Wicklow granite for the memorial.

FOUR POEMS

Anne Fitzgerald

Rituals

Seasons illuminate the familiar as new
when spring gives the cherry tree
a communion frock for a blossom.

Church spires in summertime pierce
clouds to fence with rain,
while fall brings conkers to the ground.

Yanks give thanks by eating turkeys
in mid-November, cranberries
dress their flesh in the hues of war.

A month later we slaughter these birds
with the ease that day slips into night,
to celebrate our saviour's arrival

in the way that all things
come from something else.

Uses of Water

Drinking this liquid
we absorb its purity
into our daily Sahara.
It consecrates wine
and cleanses the oasis
of our pleasures.

BOUNDARIES OF A HINTERLAND

Accents and rain claim our environs.
A bachelor builds walls
with ancestral hands. Stones touch
in the knowledge of gaps:
of female flesh or of all the children
he might have had. A field
is enclosed in his stone signature.
Weather and trespassers enter,
insects and moss shall inherit
his kingdom of fossils. Speech
from the sky pushes wild violets up.

EARLY ARRIVAL

She swims out
as a swift stone
skimming the sea

beyond starfish
and sea-horses,
beyond return.

Forward tides
iron out ebbing
idiosyncrasies.

Garments on a beach
are evidence of her
faithful departure.

FROM COME DANCE WITH ME

Ninette de Valois

Ireland in the first years of the century can only be portrayed if the reader will accept the youthful mind as I shall endeavour to recall it. A child has his own values, and his preoccupation with matters of trivial importance may play a part in the creating of an impression of the weaving of a pattern.

How can I record that time spent under the Wicklow Hills? Trivial indeed my pictures may seem to others, yet for me these pictures are intensely real; a great deal nearer to reality than much of my later life spent in the theatre.

I was born on 6 June 1898 and christened Edris (my family name is Stannus). My home, Baltiboys, a country home situated some two miles from the village of Blessington in County Wicklow, stood on the middle of a beautiful stretch of country at the foot of the Wicklow Hills. The original house was burnt in the Rising of 1798; the house was now a long two-storied building with a spacious network of basement rooms. It was a typical Irish country house of about 1820-30, late Georgian in part, consisting of one main wing and two smaller ones.

As the firstborn of the family my elder sister was acclaimed by the ringing of the big yard bell and the lighting of a bonfire high up on the fox covert which could be seen for miles around. After her birth it was decided that all such festivities in the future should be curtailed, except in relation to the arrival of a son and heir. To the chagrin of all I was the next to enter the world, and so the bell did not ring and the prepared bonfire had to be hastily dismantled.

It was not until my ninth birthday that I heard the story and was deeply hurt. Later, when reprimanded for some misdeed, I announced that one day I might light my own bonfire.

My childhood, though, was quiet, and far removed from fulfilling ambitious dreams inspired by a sense of humiliation. I was intensely reserved and as obstinate as a mule—capable of 'the sulks' (as the nursery would say) brought to a fine art. If the situation, to my mind, warranted any extra stress, I was not above staging a hunger strike—noting with satisfaction the look of nervous apprehension in the adult eye: I was a delicate, undersized child, and this physical fact, I soon discovered, helped to heighten the dramatic impact of my action. I can only remember indulging in scrapes that risked no possibility of discovery, for to do anything that might result in detection and punishment struck me as a complete waste of time. My sister had quite a different philosophy; for her the game was always worth the candle, and consequently she was regarded as headstrong and her smaller sister as deceitful.

I have an early impression of an occasional savage contempt for adult reasoning and habits, and of controlling a surge of temper over correction or dictatorial reasoning. I can also recollect a fastidious reaction to grown-up speech and accents. At one time I suffered a nightly rage directed towards a kindly English nurse; to this harmless being I had to say my prayers. The anger was caused because she would say 'Please Gawd'; I could not stand this mispronunciation, and there I knelt, hands together, eyes closed, longing to hit her; in despair one night I murmured: 'Oh God, get rid of her.'

As a nervous child, an accusation first frightened me, and as a reserved child it then humiliated me; finally my obstinacy developed a false pride, with the result that I went through an untruthful stage; oddly enough I can remember that this upset me in relation to myself, as much as it worried those in charge of me. But slowly temper would rise at the inquisition of nurses and governesses; I lied, and without a prick of conscience; the reaction of a young mind that felt the indignity and humiliation of the whole proceedings.

FROM THE STEWARD OF CHRISTENDOM

Sebastian Barry

Sebastian Barry's play The Steward of Christendom *centres on the figure of Thomas Dunne, a former Chief Superintendent of the Dublin Metropolitan Police, and now, in his seventies, an inmate of the county home in Baltinglass.*

THOMAS: My poor son... When I was a small child, smaller than yourself, my Ma Ma brought me home a red fire engine from Baltinglass. It was wrapped in the newspaper and hid in the hayshed for the Christmas. But I knew every nook and cranny of the hayshed, and I soon had it found, and the paper off it. And quite shortly I had invented a grand game, where I stood one foot on the engine and propelled myself across the yard. I kept falling and falling, tearing and scumming my clothes, but no matter, the game was a splendid game. And my mother she came out for something, maybe to fling the grain at the hens in that evening time, and she saw me skating on the engine and she looked at me. She looked with a terrible long face, and I looked down and there was the lovely engine all scratched and bent, and the wheel half-rubbed off it. So she took the toy quietly from under my foot, and marched over to the dunghill and shoved it in deep with her bare hands, tearing at the rubbish there and the layers of dung. So I sought out her favourite laying hen and put a yard-bucket over it, and it wasn't found for a week, by which time the Christmas was over and the poor hen's wits had gone astray from hunger and darkness and inertia. Nor did it ever lay eggs again that quickened with chicks. And that was a black time between my Ma Ma and me. *(After a little.)* You were six when your Mam died, Willie. Hardly enough time to be at war with her, the way a son might. She was very attached to you. Her son. She had a special way of talking about you, a special music in her voice. And she was proud of your singing, and knew you could make a go of it, in the halls, if you wished. I wanted to kill her when she said that. But at six you sang like a linnet, true enough. *(After a little.)* I didn't do as well as she did, with you. I was sorry you never reached six feet. I was a fool. What big loud talking fools are fathers sometimes. Why do we not love our sons simply and be done with it? She did. I would kill, or I would do a great thing, just to see you once more, in the flesh. All I got back was your uniform, with mud only half-washed out of it. Why do they send the uniforms to the fathers and the mothers? I put it over my head and cried for a night, like an owl in a tree. I cried for a night with your uniform over my head, and no one saw me.

FROM THE MEMORIES OF WILLIAM HANBIDGE

William Hanbidge

I will here write a short account of Stratford on Slaney
Its people and their employment
It was about three miles from my old home built on the side of a hill so that it stood on high ground in the midst of an agricultural district.
It was more noted for a cotton manufactory carried on by a Mr Orr who employed large numbers of cotton weavers with their fly shuttles, also bleachers, cutters and printers
A Mr Burnside designed all the patterns
A Mr Glynn engraved them and young men of the town were taught to cut the blocks which the printers used in stamping the calico.
But after it being woven it was bleached before it was sent to the printers.
Mr Orr shipped the greatest part to South America
Stratford was a very busy place
There were two markets held in it weekly one on Wednesday, the other on Saturday to which the surrounding farmers sent potatoes.
The butchers of Donard brought meat, but a drawback on the trade was that the buyers used to pay in Mr Orr's IOU's which readily passed in Baltinglass.
Stratford was a prosperous little place but it was also a most abominable wicked place
The scenes to be seen of a Saturday night and on Sundays were awful. Drunkenness, prostitution, cursing and fighting.
There were always a wordy warfare carried on between the country and town lads for the country lads when they saw the weavers would shout A dish of kailcannon and an iron spoon would make any calico weaver jump over his loom with other scurrilous epithets which the others resented very much.
All used to meet at a low public house about half a mile from the town on Saturday evenings and Sundays the sights which followed I cannot describe.
After a time the downfall of the town began
Mr Orr found out that he could buy the calico ready wo [*sic*] much cheaper than it cost him to have it woven so he dismissed all his weavers

who were scattered over many parts of England and Scotland

The slated houses which they lived in soon fell into ruin.

Mr Orr still continued the bleaching and printing business for a short time till his correspondent in South America failed by which he lost thousands of pounds and he turned bankrupt and could not continue the business

All the remaining employees had to seek work in England or Scotland and others such as shoemakers &c.

Thus fell Stratford   no more markets.

THE BATTLE OF BALTINGLASS

Sylvester Gaffney

O, the GPO in Dublin will go down in history,
'Twas there the glorious fight was made that set our country free:
But from Aughrim down to Boland's Mills there's nothing could surpass
The siege of the sub-Post-Office in the Town of Baltinglass.

Chorus:
There were Bren guns and Sten guns and whippet tanks galore,
The battle raging up and down from pub to gen'ral store:
Between the Vintner and the Cook the pot was quite upset,
And the Minister swore this Irish stew was the worst he ever 'et.

The job of sub-postmaster or mistress, as might be,
Is not exactly one that leads to wealth and luxury
But Korea was a picnic and Tobruk was just a pup
To the row the day the linesmen came to take the cable up.
Chorus

Now all the countryside joined in, the lowly and the great:
There were elephant-guns from Poona, and pikes from '98.
But the Cossacks came from Dublin, and the Irish navy too,
And poor cook, she burnt her fingers on this wretched Irish stew.
Chorus

There were gremlins from the Kremlin, and little men from Mars
Complete with flying saucers and hats festooned with stars.
There were rocket-firing, jet-propelled atomic flying-boats,
And Commandos from the GPO in their oul' tarpaulin coats.
Chorus

The linesmen made a dash to open up the cable trench.
They opened up the sewer instead, Lord save us! what a stench!
A gentleman in jodhpurs swore 'By Jove! they're using gas!
The next will be an atom bomb on peaceful Baltinglass!'
Chorus

Now the case has gone to UNO and we're waiting for the day
When Truman, Attlee and McBride will come along and say
'Get back behind your parallel, drop atom bombs and gas,
And respect the bound'ries and the laws of Sov'reign Baltinglass!'
Chorus

INCIDENT AT THE SCALP

Áine Miller

Today's poem is coasting
the short route to Bray.
It takes the first gradient,
Dundrum to The Mountain View,
in its stride, singing
like Catherine's sewing machine
set fair for a long seam.

From that shiny purpose
wayside cottages, blue church,
nurseries glance off; almost
too familiar to be notable, three
riders on a pony walk-out,
a child's rear windowed tongue,
the post van from Glenroe.

The road round The Scalp is new.
Wheels relish fresh grit,
humming in the lower register
this morning's theme. Cut out—
a stagger of leg and hoof, wild
eyes, nostrils, a deer out of nowhere—
thump, lurch, silence.

A faint tick-ticking from the engine,
exhalation of a chesty breath,
the hobbledy hobbledy hooves
skittery along the tarmac.

Turn the key. Edge out. Gather up
sinew for flight, a hedgerow leap
higher than the Sugarloaf.

IN THE ROCKY GLEN

Austin Clarke

Rakishly in her sports-car
Miss Mollie Garrigan
    Came round the bend
    Of the Rocky Glen,
Clapped brake on, lingered, crossed
Her legs, then lightly tossed
    A curl at us. Startled
    We saw one garter
On a thigh so radiant,
We warmed to the radiator.

Two poets, young, unwary,
What could we do but stare,
    Secretly eye it,
    Pretend the sky was
Her garage? We kept to the left
And there, with a smile, she left us,
    Drawn bow took aim
    And pinked our shame.
O was it the brat with the quiver
Who made our senses quiver?

We felt the prick, a limpid
Gaze mocking our double limp,
    How could I have guessed
    I would be the guest
Of the god, that his missile would glow
Once more in the County of Wicklow
    As I lay in bed,
    Bow-twanged, ready,
That soon with Molly beside
Me, ache would be mollified?

I heard her wash and prepare:
No need, for she was as bare
    As I was, to bolt,
    The door. Bolster
Had hidden her crepe-de-chine nightdress
Displeased by so much whiteness,
    Because in our contest
    There was nothing at all on
My handsome, my black-haired darling
Except a new pair of garters.

THREE POEMS

Nicola Lindsay

HAIKU

Earthquake

Birdsong falls silent.
All living things hold their breath
while the earth trembles.

Brockagh

Deep, in bog-brown pool,
fringed by whispering grasses,
earth-coloured trout hide.

Winter

Frost-embroidered webs.
Frozen, silver-fingered trees.
A stream, held captive.

The Hunted

Heron-hunted fish,
fearful in reed-shaded pools,
vanish in a flash.

Broken Reflections

Wind-rippled water
fragmenting the blurred whirring
of dipping mayflies.

Can You Not See?

Can you not see, that day by day,
you grow more like the man
you once resented so passionately?
The father who talked of Christ's suffering
upon the cross and who was so taken up
with thoughts of nail-torn hands and feet
and a bloodied crown of thorns
that each Passion-tide, he washed his hands
of his own family so he could better
indulge himself in his own private Calvary.

Not Superstitious

I swear I'm not superstitious but
last night the sandman didn't call
and I tossed and turned, unsleeping
and a mirror fell in the hall.

A single magpie squawked in a tree.
I spilled my salt at dinner
and the ghost that walks the gallery
has grown much sadder and thinner.

My black cat who's always near
has not been seen for days.
The gypsies have come back to the wood
and the child is lost in the maze.

There's mist on the hill and river
and the white owl calls my name.
I see her face in your dark eyes
and the moon is on the wane.

Oh, my love, I'm not superstitious
but the cards warn me of pain
and I spoke to the fortune teller—
so you do not have to explain.

FROM A FRENCHMAN'S WALK THROUGH IRELAND 1796-7

Chevalier de la Tocnaye

Generally the inhabitants of County Wicklow are very intelligent, and their country well cultivated, especially near the coasts. The low mountains and the numerous well-built houses give the district a very agreeable aspect.

I came at last to Hollybrook, where I was received by Lord Molesworth, of whose goodness I had already had experience during my sojourn at Dublin. Here laurel, arbutus, holly, and even myrtle abound, although they do not appear to fruit well, the fact being, I suppose, that to ripen berries more heat is required than is provided in this climate.

It was here that lived Robert Adair, so famous in Scotch and Irish song. I have seen his portrait; he is the ancestor of Lord Molesworth and of Sir Robert Hodson, to whom Hollybrook belongs. They told me a curious story about him. A Scotchman, a champion drunkard apparently, having heard of the Bacchic prowess of Robert Adair, came from Scotland expressly to challenge him to drink with him. He had no sooner disembarked at Dublin than he demanded from everybody he met in his Scotch jargon—'Ken ye ane Robert Adair?' and in the end he found his man. He demanded a sight of him, and gave his challenge. Robert Adair was actually at table, and offered to begin the contest there and then; but the Scotchman declined, and invited him to where all was ready at the inn in Bray.

In due time the champions appeared on the field of battle, but after ten bottles the Scotchman fell under the table. Thereupon Robert Adair rang the bell, ordered another bottle, and in presence of the domestics set himself astride the poor Scotchman, in which position he drank off the eleventh bottle without drawing breath, and gave loud huzzas for his victory.

When the Scotchman recovered he returned to his own country, but the story had preceded him, and wherever he went he was met with the mocking question, 'Ken ye ane Robert Adair?' And to this his invariable answer was 'I ken the de'il'.'

EPIPHANY IN A COUNTRY CHURCH

Sheila Wingfield

Rough-fisted winter and the blurred organ join
In minds of villagers to bring
A smell of wheatstraw under hoofs and sanfoin
In hay where beasts are fattening.

What does it matter if our wise men stress
The Barn as false, the Feast as wrong?
I hold the Magi were the wiser, yes,
To be believed in for so long.

A January mist now hides the wood;
Hard facts are overlaid by myth:
In us these last keep company, and should,
Like heart and bones in Farmer Smith.

Who kneels to pray. Rubbing his neck—If beef
Goes up this month, he thinks... Round him
Confer vague consolations, powers of grief,
Man's fear and the high cherubim.

THE WHITE ROOM

Clemency Emmet

Once I had a room in a high city tower
I painted the walls white, bare floor
A row of tall windows
The minimum of furniture.
How cold, they all said
How stark, no colour
How can you live there—

But the light was like a benediction
And the sky gave me its own colours
Luminous grey or shining blue
When the sun shone the air was gold
Filling the uncluttered room
Sunset gave me rose and orange across my walls
I had the silver glint of rain
The soft shadows of snowfall
Frost laid prisms of brightness at my windows

There in my high city tower
I was closer to the seasons
Than any country man

THE WATERFALL AT POWERSCOURT

Donald Davie

Looping off feline through the leisured air
   Water, a creature not at home in water,
Takes to the air. It comes down on its forepaws, changes
   Feet on the rockface and again extended
Bounds.   For it neither
   Pours nor is poured, but only here on the quarry
Falls at last, pours. No more the amphibious otter
   Than foundered ram can walk this water thrown
Catwalk across a further element.

Water itself is not at home in water
   But fails its creatures, as a fallen nature
Swerves from its course. And, less adaptable,
   Out of an element itself thrown out
The fallen creature cannot find itself
   Nor its own level, headlong.

Or else as a sealion, heavy and limber,
   Sedately slithers its short rock chute in the zoo
(Foolish and haughty as, propped on a stock, the Prince Regent),
   And over the water it takes to
Shoots,   so the water
   Lobs itself, immerses itself rock and, rebounding,
Surfaces smoothly backwards into space,
   Swimming the air as for freshwater miles offshore
The Orinoco dyes the ocean cold.

What end it answers, over the Sabine country
   Of Mrs Rafferty's Tusculum and Dublin's
Weekend hinterland, arching; or what use
   Insinuating underneath that ocean
Its chill of wit, who knows? The end it answers,
   The level it seeks, is its own.

TWO POEMS

Carmen Cullen

POWERSCOURT WATERFALL

The lady of the waterfall
let down her hair in sleep
and it caught in the wind and lifted,
strands of spray glistening
like dewdrop spills: diamond strings.

This was her stately gesture
from a fairy world stood still,
where millions of years are an instant
and time lasts forever
and good things reign supreme.

So we watch, while her tresses drift outward,
as though we too are in time distilled,
and the beauty of all our surroundings
shakes out human misery, baser instincts,
and makes us rich.

Bray Head

The poor ugly monster is well dead now,
or asleep for thousands of years,
since he first laid his head in the Irish sea,
having struggled to reach there
on his tiny webbed feet.

This dragon had been well dressed in green felt,
a charger for a gallant knight to ride,
snorting flames to defy all who'd face him,
the great battles over:
he grew old too, retired.

Once he was young and eager,
with a sinewy back and long tail
that blends in now with grey mountains;
his back rearing nearer:
it's Bray Head, a monster shape!

See his chin, how it rests in the sea, poor thing,
as though gently laid down there at last,
having lumbered and blundered to reach it,
across Ireland's mauve bogland
over mountains, through gaps.

Did he cry out before he lay down,
one last call, shake his head and stamp his feet?
For how could he go any further
with the ocean ahead,
his heavy body too fatigued?

Now Bray Head's no longer a monster,
just a hill, with its tip dipped in the sea,
though with houses on its side and trees and heather,
still dragon shaped enough
to seem a friend from distant years.

ENNISKERRY

Roy McFadden

Township of spires, incardinated trees,
What greeting have you for a traveller
Walking down from a war? Under your walls,
Built to define and safeguard privilege,
I think of earlier wars, and tap the stones
Hoarding their stories, and tread cobbles hoarse
From crying out against the armies. Late
Primroses at the roadside touch my feet.

Walking from war through unconscripted streets,
I turn from unapocalyptic door.
Who would reply if I demanded bread?
Of if, indeed, I asked for sanctuary?
Town of unthreatened spires, beneficent trees,
What comfort have you for a traveller
Walking from history to mythology,
And back again to darkness, where the streets,
Blacked-out at night, dream of the lamplighter?

FROM AT SALLYGAP

Mary Lavin

'We're coming near to Sallygap now,' said the conductor.

'Is that right?' said Manny. 'Give a touch to the bell so, and get the driver to stop. Anywhere here will do nicely.' He turned to the young man confidentially. 'I have to look for the place, you see.'

'I hope you find it all right, sir.'

'I hope so. Well, good day to you now. Don't forget the advice I gave you.' Manny pointed with his thumb in the direction of the sea. Then he got off the bus and for the first time in years found himself on a country road alone.

The farmhouse Manny was looking for was easy enough to find. And the farmer obligingly promised to send him down the eggs twice a week, and three times if the orders got bigger. He wanted to know if Manny ever tried selling chickens or geese? Manny said his wife took care of the orders. The farmer asked if he would mention the matter to his wife. Manny agreed to do so. They said goodbye and Manny went back to the road.

By that time Manny wanted a drink. He wasn't a drinking man, but he wanted a glass of beer just to take the thirst off him. He remembered that they had passed a public house a while before he got off the bus. He started walking back toward it.

As he walked along he thought of the boys again. It was the boat had put him in mind of them. And the young fellow that had been sitting beside him was just about the age he was himself in those days. A nice young fellow! Manny wondered who he was, and he wondered, just as idly, at what time he himself would get a bus going back to Dublin.

But it was nice, mind you, walking along the road. He didn't care if the bus was a bit slow in coming. It was not as if it was raining or cold. It was a nice evening. He'd often heard tell of young lads from Dublin coming up here on their bicycles of a fine evening, and leaving them inside a fence while they went walking in the heather. Just walking, mind you; just walking. He used to think it was a bit daft. Now that he was up here himself, he could see how a quiet sort of chap might like that sort of thing. Manny looked at the hedges that were tangled with wild vetches, and he looked at an old apple tree crocheted over with grey lichen. He looked at the gleaming grass in the wet ditch, and at the flowers and flowering reeds that grew there. They all have names, I suppose, he thought. Could you beat that!

Walking along, he soon came to a cottage with dirty brown thatch from which streaks of rain had run down the walls, leaving yellow stripes on the lime. As he got near, a woman came to the door with a black pot and swilled out a slop of green water into the road, leaving a stench of cabbage in the air when she went in. It was a queer time to be cooking her cabbage, Manny thought, and then he chuckled. 'For God's sake,' he said out loud, 'will you look at the old duck?'

A duck had flapped over from the other side of the road to see if the cabbage water made a pool big enough to swim in. 'Will you just look at him?' Manny said to himself, the road being empty. He was giving himself very superfluous advice though because he was staring at the duck as hard as he could. But as he stood there a geranium pot was taken down from inside one of the small windows of the cottage, and a face came close to the glass. They don't like you stopping and staring, I suppose, he thought, and he moved along.

IRISH BREAKFAST

Colum Kenny

The murmur of a Bray Cab at my door,
it's six a.m. and I'm still in a trance.
Out on the bypass, in through empty streets,
to Dublin airport and a flight to France.

'May all beings have happiness',
as the plane takes off.
A sense of purpose grips me when I fly,
nearer to God and stretched across the sky.

Above Bray Head I sit back in my seat,
reading the news as we gain altitude,
rising and bumping until we find our height,
an Irish breakfast as we meet the light.

The waves ran high when Wild Geese flew this way,
travelling from Ireland took time and trouble then.
Now, with my coffee drunk and papers read,
I land at Charles de Gaulle in one hour ten.

TO THE OAKS OF GLENCREE

John Millington Synge

My arms are round you, and I lean
Against you, while the lark
Sings over us, and golden lights, and green
Shadows are on your bark.

There'll come a season when you'll stretch
Black boards to cover me:
Then in Mount Jerome I will lie, poor wretch,
With worms eternally.

FROM THE NEIGHBOURHOOD OF DUBLIN

Weston St John Joyce

Glencree was in ancient times a Royal Park or preserve, almost entirely covered by primeval oak forest, and probably either wholly or partly enclosed by some description of artificial boundary to prevent the wild beasts preserved there from wandering away through the desert wilds of Wicklow. In Sweetman's Calendar it is recorded that in 1244 eighty deer were sent from the Royal forest at Chester to stock the King's park at Glencree, and that in 1296 the King sent a present to Eustace le Poer of twelve fallow deer from the Glencree forest.

As may be imagined, the repression of poaching formed no inconsiderable portion of the duties of the wardens or gamekeepers of this Royal preserve. Even the pious monks of St. Mary's Abbey, Dublin, who owned property in this neighbourhood, were unable to resist the temptation, as appears from the Chartulary of the Abbey in 1291, when the Abbot was attached for hunting in the forest with dogs and implements of the chase. In 1283 William le Deveneis, keeper of the King's demesne lands, was granted twelve oaks fit for timber from the King's wood in 'Glincry', and a few years later, Queen Eleanor, wife of Edward I, established large timber works in the valley for the purpose of providing wood for her castle, then in process of erection at Haverford. William de Moenes (one of the family from which Rathmines derives its name) was keeper and manager of these works, and judging by the accounts of his operations in the State Papers, a very considerable thinning of the Royal forest must have been effected at this period.

The Justiciary Rolls of Edward I in 1305 contain the entry of a complaint by Thomas de Sandely, a carpenter, to the effect that he was kept for three weeks in irons in the Castle of Dublin, at the suit of John Mathew, the Royal Forester at Glencree, who charged him with stealing timber. It appears that the culprit was caught in the act, but escaped and fled to Dublin, where he was arrested.

No further records of the Glencree forest can be discovered after this, and it seems probable that in consequence of the withdrawal of numbers of the English from Ireland for the purpose of the war in Scotland, and to join Edward the First's expeditions to Flanders, the forest had to be abandoned, and the Irish demolished it and its game. In any case it is pretty certain that no successful attempt could have been made to hold it during the rising of the Irish tribes and general disturbance in the country which followed the invasion of the Bruces a few years later.

At the present day, remains of the trees which composed this ancient forest are discovered in the bogs near Lough Bray, as well as on the slopes of the high hills in its neighbourhood. Of course, the Glencree forests formed only a small part of the wide-spreading forests alluded to by Holinshed and Spenser, who tell us that Wicklow glens were full of great trees on the sides of the hills, and that these forests were interspersed with goodly valleys fit for fair habitations.

In the earlier days of the English occupation, when the tyrannical laws of the Normans were rigidly enforced, and the passion for the chase displaced all other considerations, the preservation of the natural forests became an important function of the Government. But at a later period the authorities viewed with anything but a friendly eye these great tracts of forest, on account of the shelter they afforded to the troublesome 'wood kerne', and in the State Papers the woods are described as 'a shelter for all ill-disposed' and 'the seat and nursery of rebellion'. After numerous plans had been suggested for the destruction of the woods, the Government at length adopted the surest and most profitable one, namely, the establishment of iron works in all the great forest district.

A SKIMMING STONE, LOUGH BRAY

David Wheatley

   Skim a stone
   across the lake surface,
marrying water and air:
   turn this brick
   of earth, while it flies,
from stone to living fire.

   From stone to living
   fire ablaze
on the lake's faceted skin—
   tideless, the plaything
   of wind and rain,
as now of this skimmed stone.

   Watch the stone brush
   the water beneath it
and never fall below,
   dip for an instant,
   rise again
and glide like so, like so.

   Hear it echo back
   each new contact,
brushing against the surface,
   like a whip cracked
   from shore to shore
of this walled-in, echoing place.

   Skim a stone
   across the lake surface,
never suspect it may fall—
   as long as there's water
   left to walk on,
air for its echo to fill.

LOUGH BRAY

Standish O'Grady

Now Memory, false, spendthrift Memory,
Disloyal treasure-keeper of the Soul
This vision change shall never wring from thee
Nor wasteful years effacing as they roll,
O steel-blue lake, high-cradled in the hills!
O sad waves filled with little sobs and cries!
White glistening shingle, hiss of mountain rills,
And granite-hearted walls blotting the skies,
Shine, sob, gleam, gloom for ever. Oh, in me,
Be what you are in nature—a recess—
To sadness dedicate and mystery,
Withdrawn, afar, in the Soul's wilderness.
Still let my thoughts, leaving the worldly roar
Like pilgrims, wander on thy haunted shore.

PIPING IN WICKLOW

Breandán Breathnach

In modern times Wicklow has produced many exceptional traditional musicians, including the great uilleann pipers Johnny and Felix Doran from Rathnew. As Breandán Breathnach shows in this essay, however, Wicklow piping dates back to earliest times.

John Cash, of whom more later, is the hero of a song about Mick the Dalty's Ball which was once popular in Wicklow and Wexford:

> My name is Cash the piper and I'm seen at race and fair;
> I'm known to all the jolly souls from Wicklow to Kildare.

The ball in question took place in Glendalough:

> And when the ball was over the dancers all sat down;
> In tumblers, tins and teacups the punch went steaming round;
> While rough and ready Hugh stood up and sang the Ould Plaid Shawl,
> Which brought three cheers with laughter loud at Mick the Dalty's ball.

Pipers are involved in at least two placenames in the county. A prehistoric circle of stones at Athgreany is known as the Pipers Stones. Liam Price in his *Placenames of Co. Wicklow* writes that if Athgreany is correctly rendered in Irish as Achadh Gréine—the field of the sun—it may preserve some tradition of ancient religious rites. A similar placename occurred near Blessington. When the Ordnance Survey work was under way in the last century a circle of large unchiselled stones having their ends well secured in the ground was noted. A new road was subsequently driven through its centre and later the stones were used for local building. The explanation given in folk lore for the naming of these circles of stones is that music played on the pipes by the good people could be heard in them. There is little doubt that the name does not derive from terrestrial pipers.

From history we come to the devastating reign of the first Elizabeth. The background to our references is found in the savage and unrelenting campaign waged by the English government against the O'Byrnes. Its nature may be gauged from the directions given in 1579 to Sir Henry Harrington when he was appointed seneschal and chief ruler of the O'Byrne country. He was on his appointment instructed to issue a proclamation that no idle person, vagabond, or masterless man, bard, rymor or other notorious malefactor remain within the district on pain of whipping after eight days, and on pain of death after twenty days. Harpers and pipers were included under the general term of malefactor. Some years previously the Lord Deputy had written from Dublin to Elizabeth complaining that Fiach Mac Aodha Ó Broin, Ruairí óg Ó Mórdha and other rebels were so disdainful of the weakened defences of the Pale that they came on their raids headed by pipers in the daytime and by torchbearers at night; they were not concerned in any way to hide their approach. Tradition has it that 'Follow me down to Carlow' was the clan march of the O'Byrnes and that it was first performed by the pipers of Fiach when attacking the English of the Pale in 1590. How trustworthy that tradition is I am unable to say.

The Image of Ireland, a work published in 1581, is a versified account of the war waged by the Lord Deputy, Sir Henry Sidney, Enrí na Beorach he was called by the Irish, against Ruairí Ó Mórdha. The modern edition contains a series of woodcuts depicting events in this campaign and experts are agreed that they were drawn by an eye-witness. One represents a raid on the Pale by a band of 'wilde woodkarne' headed by a piper. Another shows an engagement between the Irish and the English in which attention is drawn to the figure of a piper who has been slain, in this way pointing out the importance of the incident. Ó Mórdha's wife, Margaret, was a daughter of Fiach Mac Aoidh and she and a number of other women and children were slaughtered at the instigation of Sidney. When the county was finally pacified fiants or pardons were issued in favour of some of the Queen's enemies. The fiant pardoning Phelim, son of Fiach, dated 24 September 1601, included Cahell m'Ekelle, Donogh and Donell, pipers. It is interesting to observe that Phelim O'Byrne is described as being of Ballincor, Co. Dublin. Wicklow had not yet emerged as a separate county. A pardon dated 15 May 1601, in favour of Donell Spaynagh Kavanagh of Clonemullin, included Brene m'Gyllechriste, Patr oge O Ferrayle and Fergasse O Ferrayle, pipers. Also near enough to our scene to be mentioned here is Owen, a piper from Karrickmayne, who was pardoned some years before this time.

THE COW ATE THE PIPER

Anon.

In the year ninety-eight, when our troubles were great,
It was treason to be a Milesian.
I can never forget the big black whiskered set
That history tells us were Hessians.
In them heart breaking times we had all sorts of crimes,
As murder never was rifer.
On the hill of Glencree not an acre from me,
Lived bould Denny Byrne, the piper.

Neither wedding nor wake was worth an old shake,
If Denny was not first invited.
For at emptying kegs or squeezing the bags
He astonished as well as delighted.
In such times poor Denny could not earn a penny,
Martial law had a sting like a viper—
It kept Denny within till his bones and his skin
Were a-grin through the rags of the piper.

'Twas one heavenly night, with the moon shining bright,
Coming home from the fair of Rathangan,
He happened to see, from the branch of a tree,
The corpse of a Hessian there hanging;
Says Denny, 'These rogues have fine boots, I've no brogues',
He laid on the heels such a griper,
They were so gallus tight, and he pulled with such might,
Legs and boots came away with the piper.

So he tucked up the legs and he took to his pegs,
Till he came to Tim Kavanagh's cabin,
'By the powers', says Tim, 'I can't let you in,
You'll be shot if you stop out there rappin'.'
He went round to the shed, where the cow was in bed,
With a wisp he began for to wipe for—

They lay down together on the seven foot heather,
And the cow fell a-hugging the piper.

The daylight soon dawned, Denny got up and yawned,
Then he dragged on the boots of the Hessian:
The legs, by the law! he threw them on the straw,
And he gave them leg-bail on his mission.
When Tim's breakfast was done he sent out his son
To make Denny lep like a lamp-lighter—
When two legs there he saw, he roared like a daw
   'Oh! daddy, de cow eat de piper.'

'Sweet bad luck to the beast, she'd a musical taste,'
Says Tim, 'to go eat such a chanter,
Here Pádraic, avic, take this lump of a stick,
Drive her up to Glenealy, I'll cant her.'
Mrs Kavanagh bawled—the neighbours were called,
They began for to humbug and jibe her,
To the churchyard she walks with the legs in a box,
Crying out, 'We'll be hanged for the piper.'

The cow then was drove just a mile or two off,
To a fair by the side of Glenealy,
And the crathur was sold for four guineas in gold
To the clerk of the parish, Tim Daly.
They went into a tent, and the luck-penny spent
(For the clerk was a woeful old swiper),
Who the divil was there, playing the Rakes of Kildare,
But their friend, Denny Byrne, the piper.

Then Tim gave a bolt like a half-broken colt,
At the piper he gazed like a gommach;
Says he, 'By the powers, I thought these eight hours,
You were playing in Dhrimindhu's stomach.'
But Denny observed how the Hessian was served,
So they all wished Nick's cure to the viper,
And for grá that they met, their whistles they wet,
And like devils they danced round the piper.

FROM WAKING

Hugh Maxton

On the other side of the Tinakilly road, Bob Lawrence had established semi-independence from Culahullin, raising turkeys for the Christmas market and allowing a few sheep the run of his back fields. Though he held afternoon court in a nicely modernised kitchen under a corrugated iron roof, he returned each night to sleep in the old thatched cottage with his brothers and unmarried sister. He was very big, strong but stiff, with massive hands: and the fine dust of hen-shit and straw clung to his thick worsted trousers. Standing he dominated me, seated by the fire he unrolled story after enchanting story, interspersing these local narratives with questions to me which I could never answer to my own satisfaction. The inquiries themselves had long preambles—'what would you say to the notion of... how would a man ever get the hang of...?' The side of the farm slid upward to where granite had been quarried for Liverpool cathedral—or was it Westminster?—and the entire area bounded by the name-correcting woods was cradled in the safe hollow of the word 'would'. Bob's stories often complemented Uncle Jimmy's, for Jimmy would feature as a character in Bob's, and the circle closed delightedly on my ear.

But his best story lay back in the troubled past, and he drew it forth for me only twice. He had been blasting stones in Ballymorris all day, and returning somehow through Aughrim he stopped off at Lawless's to slake the dust out of his throat. Bob was a teetotaller all his life, and a mineral sufficed, together with copious slow talk with men leaning one hip on the worn counter. Doubtless the bushman saw, the smoked ham, and the raw leather boots hung down over the ritual phrases like commonplace items of sacrifice, purchased on the harvest or the potatoes of another season. The conversation of that evening he never recreated in any detail, for a story has its unspoken wavelength also, just as a question finishes many an answer. When the Black and Tans arrived suddenly in front of the hotel, there was no time for anyone to slip away or to hive off from suspect acquaintances. Bob breathed to his neighbour, 'I'm done for, I've the remains of dynamite in my pocket.' The Tans advanced down the bar, throwing this one or that across the bar to be rummaged and searched.

When they were two paces or one away from Bob, his neighbour broke out in execration heightened in the Wicklow whine of the man then and Bob telling it forty years later—'no point searchin' the fuckin' Protestant fuckin' bastard, ahny hoaw, fur he's fuckin' one of yees ahny hoaw'.

I meet Cousin John, and he confirms the story. But now it is Bob's brother Jim who has the lucky escape.

FROM THE STONES OF BRAY

Canon George Digby-Scott

Unquestionably the greatest turning point in Irish history was the coming of St Patrick, with the wonderful advance in the Christianisation of the island which dates from the commencement of his mission. The spot, therefore, at which St Patrick first landed on his mission to make disciples of the Irish nation, has an intense historical interest attached to it. You can see that spot from here. Perhaps you do not know that some historians of former days, including the learned Editor of the Annals of the Four Masters, Dr O'Donovan, supposed that Bray was that spot. But now all scholars seem agreed that the river Dee in Cualann, at the mouth of which St Patrick landed, was not the Bray Water but the Vartry, and therefore it is not Bray but Wicklow that bears the honour, or shall I rather say the reproach, of having given such a bad reception to the Christian Apostle that he was obliged to leave it after a short sojourn, and to seek for a more fruitful soil in which to sow the good seed further north. It had treated his predecessor Palladius in the same way before. You see Wicklow Head and its lighthouse away down there? And can you make out the town, just where the headland breaks out from the line of the coast? That is where the mouth of the river is. There St Patrick landed in the year A.D. 432, but apparently met with the same opposition by which the work of Palladius had been thwarted. A story is told in the Annals of Clonmacnoise, that one of the Saint's companions was struck in the mouth with a stone, with the result that he lost all his front teeth, and was thenceforward called Mantan or the toothless. Apparently we are to suppose that he took a real Christian revenge, returning good for evil, and chose the scene of his injury to be the place where he became a hermit missionary; for that place came to be known as Cill-Mantain, until the Danes seized it, as they did all the good harbours, and called it after themselves Wykynglo.

FROM PARNELL: A MEMOIR

Edward Byrne

Charles Stewart Parnell (1846-1891) was the greatest Irish politician of the late nineteenth century, and the leader of the Irish Party in Westminster. He was also a Wicklowman, with a family home in Avondale near Rathdrum. In 1888 the London Times *accused him of complicity in the Phoenix Park murders of 1882, on the forged evidence of Richard Pigott. This extract from Edward Byrne's memoir, describing a visit to Parnell at his hunting lodge in Aughavannagh, shows his characteristically fighting response.*

I remember when the *Times* Commission, otherwise the impeachment of Parnell, was pending, I interviewed him at Aughavannagh during the grouse season. My wife and I went down the previous evening and slept in the hotel at the foot of the mountain, whence we dropped up to the barracks built to put down the outlaw, Michael Dwyer, and then occupied by the man regarded in millions of English hearts as not less an outlaw who was to be crushed by fair means or foul, by Pigott's forgery or open force. When the car upon which we drove reached the old swing-gate opening on the barracks, we were met by a sort of gamekeeper, tall, suspicious-visaged, and deterrent, with a shaggy, savage-looking dog at his heels of the half-breed cur kind so frequent in Irish villages and so snappish and vicious. I saluted the man; he scowled; the dog growled. Two omens! I asked the human custodian of the place 'Is Mr Parnell at home?' He growled out bluntly, not less ominously than had his attendant spirit, that he was not. I ventured to remark that that was strange, as I had an appointment with him. A change of expression came over the janitor's face, but still it was distrustful. The dog also brightened up; his sour muzzle somewhat softened its surliness, and there actually seemed an indication that that appendage which is euphemized as the hairy index of the canine mind, would wag. At this moment my then youngish eyes discerned a figure descending the mountain mounted on a heavy-looking horse, with game-bags straddled across the animal's shoulders. 'That's Mr Parnell,' said I, 'coming down there after a shoot.' 'Oh! you know him, then,' said the keeper, 'are you—?' I am,' replied I, jumping off the car—for the original expressions on my receivers' faces had relaxed—and running through the gate towards Mr

Parnell, who was very pleased to see me, and showed it in his best form. The first thing he said, after the usual greetings, was—'I suppose you think these bags filled with grouse. They are not. I hardly ever shoot now. I don't care for it. The others are up the mountain. I have been picking ore. These are specimens. They contain gold [handing me one out of the contents of the bag], as you may see.'

The stone did sparkle like

'our Lagenian mine.

The tiny glittering specks

'… over the surface shine!'

We, three, the lady, he, and I, entered the barracks or lodge, and, ascending the rugged stairs, came to a large roomy apartment in the middle of which was an oval table strewn all over, or, rather, littered with papers or letters in a by no means sweet disorder. We chatted pleasantly on various topics for some time, Mr Parnell became most unusually voluble. His simplicity of character gleamed out, for instance, when a question arose. I am under the middle height. Either my wife, who is tall, or I asked him what height he was. I am six feet, he answered, with a faint radiancy of innocent pride in his eye, and, suiting the action to the word, he stood up and, asking the lady to rise, they put back to back, and, knowing her height, I measured the difference and found Mr Parnell a little over six feet. He would be six feet in his stockings. After lunch, which was a most rustic *mélange*, ham and grouse and domestic fowl and fruit and tea and wine and whiskey, taken from the window embrasures and queer recesses with all sorts and conditions of china and plate and glass, we, he and I, began to talk business. At this time everything looked as black and gloomy as they well could. Imagine my surprise when, beginning an interview, which was to appear in the then leading newspaper of Ireland, of which I was editor, the next morning, the patriot, practically impeached for murder and high treason, said, 'Write we will open thus: "Before a week of the Commission has expired, Mr McDonald, the manager of *The Times* will be in the dock."'

'It is true, though,' he retorted, 'begin as I say.' The interview proceeded. It appeared in the newspaper already alluded to, the next morning, my wife and I having returned to Dublin that night. But I excised the opening sentence, which he had stuck to. I judged it too strong for general consumption at the juncture. I preferred and deemed it better, in the temper of time, to let matters develop themselves. But Mr Parnell, *mens conscia recti*, was confident and bold.

Long after, when he was the master of the very masses that had thirsted for his blood, he and I were together—indeed it was, if I recall aright, on our way to Hawarden—he suddenly turned towards me and said—'Why did you not publish the opening sentence at that interview which I gave you at Aughavannagh before the *Times* commission?' He repeated it word for word. It was one of his singular characteristics that he remembered, liberatim or verbatim, what he said on the many occasions when I interviewed him, as if he had arranged and shelved in his lucid brain the whole statement ready for use and after reference, his words being carefully selected with no redundancy, with directness straight as a die.

I said in extenuation, so to speak, what I had urged on the eve of the appearance of the very remarkable and very momentous interview. He mildly retorted, 'You see, I was right.' 'Well,' I acknowledged, 'if you were not exactly right, you were very near it; if Mr McDonald, the manager of *The Times*, who bought the forged letter from Pigott, was not in the dock, he deserved to be.'

THE BLACKBIRD OF SWEET AVONDALE

Anon

By the sweet bay of Dublin whilst carelessly straying
I sat myself down by a green myrtle shade
Reclined on the beach as the wild waves were rolling
In sorrow condoling I saw a fair maid.

Her robes changed to mourning that once were so glorious
I stood in amazement to hear her sad wail.
Her heart strings burst out in wild accents uproarious
Saying, where is my Blackbird of sweet Avondale?

The fowlers waylaid him in hopes to ensnare him
While I here in sadness his absence bewail,
And it grieves me to think that the walls of Kilmainham
Surround my poor blackbird of sweet Avondale.

O Erin my country awake from your slumbers
And bring back my blackbird so dear unto me
Let everyone know by the strength of your numbers
That we as a nation would like to be free.

The cold prison dungeon is no habitation
For one to his country so loyal and true
So give him his freedom without hesitation
Remember he fought hard for freedom and you.

The linnet and thrush in sadness may wander
It grieves me at eve to hear their sad tone,
But the thought of my blackbird often drives me to madness
Since I must sit here in sorrow alone.

The birds of the forest for me have no charm
Not even the voice of the sweetest nightingale,
Her notes so charming fill my heart with alarm
Since I lost my poor blackbird of sweet Avondale.

O heaven! Give ear to my supplication
And strengthen the bold sons of old Grainne Mhaoil
And grant that my country will soon be a nation
And bring back my blackbird to sweet Avondale.

FROM SILENT YEARS

J.F. Byrne

Pertaining to the notion of the occult, or of auto-suggestion, or maybe, hypnosis, is a simple story I heard as a boy from gaffer Fogarty. He said that when he was a boy of about twelve years old, he saw one day, after a fair in Rathdrum, a ring of people on the fairgreen surrounding three roving jugglers and entertainers; the three being ostensibly father, mother, and a young boy, their son. When the trio had exhausted their bag of tricks, the father asked the assembled audience would they like to know what the weather was going to be during the next few days; if they would, he said, he would send the lad up to find out. Of course the ring of spectators were all for knowing about the future weather, and when the man passed the hat, they contributed generously. The collection having been made, the man took a cotton ball out of his pocket, and holding the end of the thread in his fingers, he tossed the ball away up until it disappeared from sight. Then pointing to the thread suspended from the sky, he said to the boy: 'Here, you, climb up and see what kind of weather we're going to have.' To the amazement of the surrounding circle of gazers, the boy clambered rapidly, hand over hand, up the cotton thread until he disappeared into the sky. The man and wife continued their palaver for a while, and then the man said to the woman, 'I wonder what's keeping sonny up there. Maybe he's lost, you'd better go up and look for him.' And this the woman proceeded to do, as she, unlike the boy, climbed up slowly, hand over hand, till she, too, disappeared in the heavens. The man chattered idly for a couple of minutes and then he began to worry about his son and wife, neither of whom had reappeared. 'I don't know what's become of them' he wailed, 'maybe they've both got lost, I'll have to go up and see.'

So up he went, climbing even faster than the boy; and as he ascended he took the cotton thread up with him, and he disappeared from view. The spellbound circle of spectators stood for maybe ten minutes craning their necks, and then a farmer who was driving into town asked what was up. He was told excitedly, 'Three people are up—up there.' 'Up where,' he says. And still the crowd pointed to the sky. 'What d'ye mane—three people gone up there—gone up where—are y'all gone mad!'

Then a few of the crowd came to him and told him about the three ascensionists, and what they had been doing—and described them. 'My God,' said the farmer, blessing himself, 'tis only too thrue—ye're all turned into lunatics. Why I met the three o' them—man, woman and boy—only five or six minutes ago walking on the road towards Greenan.'

FROM AN IRISH UTOPIA

John H. Edge

The Vale of Clara extends from Laragh Bridge, near Glendalough, to the town of Rathdrum. It is one of the loveliest of the many lovely vales of beautiful Wicklow.

Rathdrum is a town in Ireland; it would be merely a village in England.

The Avonmore, or big Avon, flows out of the lakes of Glendalough, and runs along the Vale the whole way, passes Rathdrum and Avondale—and joins the Avonbeg, or little Avon, at the Meeting of the Waters, which inspired one of the sweetest of Moore's Irish Melodies.

From Rathdrum to the sea the Vale is called the Vale of Avoca; and the double stream from the Meeting of the Waters is known as the Avoca river.

The scenery of County Wicklow cannot be so easily described as that of Switzerland. There are no such startling surprises in Wicklow as in Switzerland—no snow-clad mountains or glaciers, contrasting strongly with pine-woods, rich pastures, edelweiss, and wild flowers; yet Wicklow scenery has its own distinctive charms. In spring or summer, more especially in bright sunshine after rain, no more delightful excursion could be taken than from Rathdrum through the Vale of Clara to Glendalough, either by car, carriage, or motor-car, or on foot or cycling, though the road is somewhat hilly. If the valley from Rathdrum down by the river to the sea at Arklow is better wooded and more luxuriantly beautiful, the view, about five or six miles from Rathdrum, in Clara Vale, where Clara Bridge suddenly comes into sight, is grander than anything in the Vale of Avoca.

About half a mile further on and above the road are the ruins of the castle of the MacU'Thuils, or MacTooles, or O'Tooles, who for many years were the masters, if not strictly in law, certainly in fact, of all this mountainous region. Another castle beyond Laragh Bridge near Annamoe disputes the glory of having been the stronghold of this once powerful sept. The ruins of the castle at Annamoe are curiously called Castle Kevin, whilst the ruins in the Vale of Clara are known locally as King O'Toole's Castle; and the townland on which it stands Knockreagh, or King's Hill, corrupted into Knockrath. Probably both castles were fortresses against the English enemy, and were occupied by the king according to the necessity of the times.

A mile or two higher up than the castle, and near the heather on the wild mountain called the Castle Hill, was erected in the seventeenth century a large Irish country house, built, as the greater number of such houses were, of the massive stone of the district, quite regardless of architectural effect, three storeys high, with a basement storey, and the hall-door in the centre. The demesne, or home-farm surrounding the house, had a few oaks and ash-trees, and little ornamentation. This house was built by Michael Corbet, a captain in Cromwell's army, who got a Crown grant of the forfeited estates in the valley. He, having little means or assistance, built this house, bounded off a farm round it, and set some portions of the rest of the lands on long leases to his soldiers, who paid him small rents, and acted as his bodyguard against the so-called wild Irish. The greater part of the lands contained in Corbet's grant remained unoccupied and waste until the close of the eighteenth or beginning of the nineteenth century, when wheat rose to a great price after the American war, and during the wars of the First Napoleon.

ROOF-TREE

Richard Murphy

After you brought her home with your first child
How did you celebrate? Not with a poem
She might have loved, but orders to rebuild
The house. Men tore me open, room by room.

Your daughter's cries were answered by loud cracks
Of hammers stripping slates; the clawing down
Of dozed rafters; dull, stupefying knocks
On walls. Proudly your hackwork made me groan.

Your greed for kiln-dried oak that could outlast
Seven generations broke her heart. My mind
You filled with rot-proof hemlock at a cost
That killed her love. The dust spread unrefined.

To renovate my structure, which survives,
You flawed the tenderest movement of three lives.

LUGGALA

John Montague

Again and again in dream, I return to that shore. There is a wind rising, a gull is trying to skim over the pines, and the waves whisper and strike along the bright sickle of the little strand. Slowing through reeds and rushes, leaping over a bogbrown stream, I approach the temple by the water's edge, death's shrine, cornerstone of your sadness. I stand inside, by one of the pillars of the mausoleum, and watch the water in the stone basin. As the wind ruffles cease, a calm surface appears, like a mirror or crystal. And into it your face rises, sad beyond speech, sad with an acceptance of blind, implacable process. For by this grey temple are three tombs, a baby brother, a half-sister and a grown brother, killed at twenty-one. Their monuments of Wicklow granite are as natural here as the scattered rocks, but there is no promise of resurrection, only the ultimate silence of the place, the shale littered face of the scree, the dark, dark waters of the glacial lake.

SOME WICKLOW WORDS

Diarmaid Ó Muirithe

When a Wicklow man cleans out or disembowels a rabbit, he panches him. This word was known also to Colm Devereux of the Willow Grove and to Michael Donnelly of Corrigower, but not to two young ones of about 20 who sipped a drink in Mr Devereux's pub. Bad news this. I didn't bother asking them what they'd do to a deer; you wouldn't panch it, you'd grollick it in both Rathdrum and Callary. This is from Irish *greallach,* entrails. Scots Gaelic has the word too; and Scots English has gralloch.

George Mooney from Newtownmountkennedy gave me the word *shoorawns,* and Father Mac Cárthaigh knows of a woman who had, unwisely, cut them with a strimmer and suffered a severe rash as a consequence of being hit by flying pieces of the weed known to most of us as hogweed or cow-parsnip.

The Wicklow Irish is *siúrán.* De Bhaldraithe's dictionary gives *odhrán;* McKenna's has *odhrán, feabhrán, fuarán* and *fleabhrán*; and Dinneen found *fiúrán* in Dublin, a word sent to me in the form *fewrawn* by J. O'Brien of Shankill some time ago.

Cloerauns is another of Michael Donnelly's words. They are heaps of small stones gathered from a cornfield to assist the mower; the cairns are usually built near the ditches in the corner of the field. The word, no doubt, is a local form of Irish *clochrán.*

Lastly, an old use of the word *concern* from Wicklow. I heard it at young Geraldine Magee's wedding the other night. A woman who lives near Geraldine in Corrigower was talking about President Clinton's *concern.* This was her word for an affair. It was a common euphemism in Restoration days.

'It is not long ago that I had a concern with a signora,' wrote the dramatist Wilson in *Bolphegor* in 1690. Obsolete everywhere now, Oxford thinks. Tell them that in Wicklow.

The Irish Times, 29 August 1998

SUNDAY LUNCH

Marie O'Nolan

Three people, a man and two women, are seated at a table in the centre of the room. Although the dining room of the country house hotel is crowded and noisy with conversation, they are momentarily frozen in silence and perhaps because of this, look as if they had always been there.

This, in a sense, is true. They come here often on a Sunday, these three, and are always given the same table. It is a circular one which looks as if it could accommodate more people, which also, in a sense, it does, perhaps the people that they once were.

Bernard and Mollie have been married for twenty-six years. They had, the previous year, passed the quarter of a century signpost of their years together, which had been marked with all the appropriate celebrations by family and friends. It had been like the apex of a curve on a chart which had now begun to slant imperceptibly downwards.

Kate is unmarried and is a lifelong friend of Mollie's. They had been at school together and had many shared interests, including Bernard. Before he had married Mollie, he had been engaged, briefly, to Kate.

The waitress comes to take their order and they seem suddenly to animate, like a picture come to life. At first it appears that there is to be nothing original about their choice of food. The waitress has almost written down what it usually is, the Wicklow lamb, when Bernard suddenly changes his mind and orders the beef.

'Why?' asks Mollie, after the girl has gone.

Bernard shrugs.

'I just feel like a change.'

But his wife does not let go.

'But the lamb is always so good here and beef doesn't always agree with you, dear.'

Bernard's eyes flicker with slight annoyance but he does not reply. Yet Mollie's remarks seem to create an uneasiness which encircles the table like a fourth presence.

'But the beef is always good too,' interjects Kate quickly, 'I had it last week.'

Mollie's eyebrows arch in surprise, or is it slight annoyance?

'You were here last week. Who with?'

'A colleague,' replies Kate with a faint flush of embarrassment.

'Male or female?' her friend insists.

'Mollie, that's her business,' Bernard interrupts as the wine arrives. The waitress pours some into his glass. He tests it and nods to her but indicates that he will pour it himself.

'I was only interested,' murmurs Mollie after the ritual is over.

The subject is dropped and they relapse into silence again as Bernard fills their glasses. He pours Kate's first, filling it a little too full; he gives less to his wife and even less to himself, spilling some in the process. A faint, red stain spreads on the white tablecloth. Mollie makes a slight gesture of impatience.

'Perhaps we should put salt on it. It's good for wine stains.'

'I shouldn't bother, Mollie,' says her friend. 'I suspect wine stains are a daily occurrence here. I am sure they have a sure way of dealing with them.'

Bernard throws Kate a grateful glance but Mollie nevertheless picks up the salt shaker. She is about to pour some on the offending stain when she is distracted by their starters arriving and desists. There is no source of surprise or rancour there. Melon balls for two and a fan-shaped avocado vinaigrette for one as usual.

Bernard's engagement to Kate had been very short and had been ended abruptly by her. It now has the blandness of memory for him but for some reason he can still remember the moving shadows in the room the day she told him she could not marry him. It was raining and the reflections from the window had played on her face, making the image come and go before his eyes. She has changed very little in twenty odd years, he thinks, much less than Mollie who had once been the prettier of the two. Kate's face has grown into her character. With Mollie it is the opposite. Not that he had any regrets really…

When their main courses arrive there is a slight tension, but Mollie does not make any further comment, though she passes him the horseradish sauce in a slightly marked manner. She helps Kate and herself to the mint sauce. She then returns to the subject of Kate's escort of a week ago. Bernard does not try to dissuade her this time. He even joins in the speculation.

'It was only Tom Blake,' Kate admits finally.

'No man would like to be described in those terms,' Bernard comments dryly. 'At least I wouldn't.'

Kate flushes again slightly and looks at him.

'Sorry. I didn't mean that the way it sounded.'

'I think you did,' says Mollie, 'and I don't blame you. If ever a man was "only", Tom Blake is.'

'He has his good points,' qualifies Kate.

'If you are driven to counting his good points, he must really leave you cold,' finishes Mollie.

All three laugh and the subject is dropped, except perhaps in their minds.

As she cuts into her lamb Kate recalls her lunch with Tom Blake. It had been an unexpected invitation and its purpose even more unforeseen. Half-way through the meal, without preliminaries, he had asked her to marry him. She had known and worked in his firm for many years, sympathised with him on the death of his wife, two years ago, even advised him about schools for his children, but he had never given her any indication of having feelings for her other than friendship. They had had drinks together many times after business meetings but it had always been on an impersonal level, or so it had seemed to her. If she had had warning of his proposal she would probably have refused it outright but, taken aback as she had been, instead she had told him she would think about it and let him know. She had wondered on the way to lunch with her friends that day if she should ask Mollie's advice, but it seemed that it had already been given.

The choice of the third course presents no problem either. Apple tart for Mollie, crème caramel for Kate and selections from the cheese board for Bernard. The dining room is emptying around them as they are slow eaters. Besides, they had been a little late in arriving owing to a phone call from one of Mollie and Bernard's boys at university. The round table in the middle seems even more isolated in time. Conversation has become more general again when the waitress comes and asks them if they would prefer coffee in the lounge or the garden.

'The lounge, I think,' replies Mollie, answering for all.

'It's fine enough for the garden, surely,' suggests Bernard, peering through the window.

'But there is an east wind,' Mollie points out. 'What do you think, Kate?'

Kate raises her shoulders indifferently. She would have preferred the garden too but did not want to add to the obvious tension. Besides, she has her own problems.

'Why not let her serve it to us in the lounge and Bernard can take his cup into the garden if he wishes,' she compromises amicably, if a little wearily.

'You should have joined the diplomatic service,' remarks Mollie a trifle dryly after the waitress has taken the order.

Bernard grimaces in Kate's direction as they rise from the table.

Kate is asking how the boys are doing at university when the coffee is brought to the long, low-ceilinged lounge. One of them is her godson. They sit at a small table close to a window. A branch of a climbing tree taps against one of the panes in a harmonious monotony. Bernard does not take his cup to the garden as Kate suggested nor does he join in the conversation about his sons. Instead he remains seated in silence. It is left to Mollie to answer Kate's inquiries, which open up a new avenue of tension.

'One worries about the young these days when they aren't under one's eyes,' finishes Mollie, offering more coffee. 'Drugs and sex and all that. It was different in our day.'

At this point Bernard refuses a refill of coffee and says he is going to the garden for a smoke.

'Perhaps you should take your coat, dear. The wind…' suggests Mollie, but he has gone before she has time to finish the sentence. When he is out of earshot Mollie turns to her friend, her face assuming an expression of feigned tolerance.

'A touch of mid-life crisis, I think.'

'You mean Bernard. Hardly.'

'The trouble with you, Kate dear, is that you haven't lived with him for the past twenty-six years. You still think of him as he was when he was young.'

'He isn't old and neither are you.'

'Marriage makes you old. Most institutions do. You're wise you never married.'

'But I thought you had a happy marriage.'

'Oh we are happy in a general sort of way. But the particulars have gone.'

'What do you mean, the particulars?' Kate smiles a little indulgently.

'The things you start out with, the romance, the expectations…'

'Surely what you have compensates for all that. The boys, your lovely home...'

'That isn't what I meant. Men are more romantic than women. I don't think I was ever romantic enough for Bernard. Probably you were, but you turned him down. That of course gives you a distinct advantage over me.'

Kate laughs outright.

'What advantage, for heaven's sake?'

'The advantage of the untried, the unfulfilled dream. Oscar Wilde was right.'

'About what?'

'There are two tragedies in life. One is not getting one's heart's desire–'

'The other,' finishes Kate, 'is getting it. That was just an epigram among too many epigrams. Life isn't like that. Words can delude us especially when they are clever.'

'And they can lose their meaning when they are spoken by the same people for too long. Ever since we arrived here today, I have had a feeling that he wanted to talk to you instead of me, that what you had to say would not be stale or overused.'

'Mollie, I'm sure that isn't true...'

'If I were wise I would let him. He might learn something.'

Kate looks at her friend keenly.

'Are you really serious about this?'

'Perfectly serious. I think that Bernard has got to a stage in his life when he needs to lay a few ghosts. Perhaps you are the one to help him do it.'

'What do you want me to do?'

'Go out there and talk to him.'

'What about?'

'Anything. Ask his advice about something, anything...'

'As a matter of fact I could do with some advice.'

'Oh!' She seems momentarily diverted but reverts instead. 'Then go and ask him, go... go...' She waves her hand in a gesture of dismissal.

Kate finds Bernard in the orchard standing under an apple tree. He is looking at the large number of windfalls that lie, uncollected, in a rough circle on the ground, some of them half-rotting back into the soil. The sun is dappling the turf under the tree, throwing up lights into his face. Its moving glow makes him look younger. He smiles a little sheepishly when he sees her approach.

'Sorry to be so unsociable,' he says then goes on, with his eyes focused on the strewn ground. 'She's good for me, you know. She always has been.'

'I know, Bernard.'

'The trouble is that she's right about most things but I don't always want to hear about them, not in so many words.'

'I understand.'

'Words are a little like those windfalls,' he muses, kicking one of the rotting apples with the toe of his shoe. 'Most of the crop is wasted and goes back into the melting pot of more wasted apples—or words.'

'And the words that aren't wasted?'

'They're the ones that don't need to be spoken.'

'That sounds very deep. I don't think I quite understand it.'

He does not answer and they walk away from the tree in silence. They take the path down to the river. When they arrive there, they stand for a few moments, in a different silence, watching the new water flow from under the old bridge. Suddenly, on the reedy bank he turns to her.

'Why did you turn me down, Kate? I never really understood your reason. You said at the time that it wasn't that you didn't love me but…'

'I think I realized I was not the marrying kind and I have proved that surely by not marrying.'

'But you must have had other offers, a woman like you.'

'I had one only last week as a matter of fact.'

'From Blake?'

She nods.

'What did you say to him?'

After a slight pause she tells him.

'At least you left the poor guy with some hope. That's more than you did for me.'

'Come now, Bernard, you didn't waste much time in replacing me.'

'Shall we say that you created a huge void that had to be filled.'

'It was more than that. You were mad about Mollie the day you married her. Remember, I was there. I saw it. You took scant notice of the chief bridesmaid in the pink dress.'

'Was it pink? I could have sworn it was blue,' he says lightly.

Laughing, they walk away from the river towards the circular lawn with its flowering borders and small, low, box-hedged maze. Children are playing a chasing game around the empty garden chairs.

'Will you marry him, do you think?' he asks presently as they enter the tiny maze.

'Coming here today I thought I might. Now I'm not so sure.'

'What made you change your mind?'

'You and Mollie. Both of you.'

'But I said nothing against him even if Mollie did. Besides, neither of us was a particularly good advertisement for the happy state today.'

'It wasn't what either of you said.'

'What then?'

'You made me realize that there are no rules about all this. That things go wrong and misunderstandings arise but it makes no difference to the dimension itself.'

'Are you being general or specific?'

'Both. I think that there is wasted time and there are wasted words like those apples in the orchard but in the end it is the same. They go back to nourish what is there and is to come.'

'Now who is sounding very deep?'

She smiles, then goes on. 'I think that the fundamental feeling changes but it doesn't go away. You have that with Mollie, but I don't think I would have it with Tom Blake. In fact I know I wouldn't.'

'Poor guy. I know just how he's going to feel when you tell him.'

As they come out of the maze she looks at him shrewdly.

'You don't really want me to marry anyone, do you, Bernard?' she challenges him.

He pauses before replying, his eyes resting on her face.

'That's one of the words that do not need to be spoken, Kate.'

She drops her eyes and flushes a little.

'Perhaps we should be getting back, Bernard. Mollie will want to get on the road before the light goes.'

They walk back to the hotel in silence. By the time they have come close to the side door that leads into the garden, a cold wind has sprung up. Mollie appears at the door. She is carrying their coats. They both feel already warmed by the gesture and walk towards her, smiling.

THREE POEMS

Alma Brayden

DNA

To forget
to remember to forget,
then find a white hair
hidden, like contraband,
underneath the fireside chair
moulded, vaguely, to her shape.

I'll keep it in a box
for scientists to strip
away the cells
revealing the blueprint
to remake her.

But will she be the same?
Can they recreate, precisely,
the smell of baking,
a vase of flowers reflected
on the polished table,
subtle renderings of Schubert,
a point of view that always
saw the light?

Early Walking

Small feet dance time
with father's stride
along a rutted road of mystery.
Two pilgrims on a Sunday afternoon.
His blackthorn stick, never used in anger,
indicates points of interest:
wrens and dunnocks, a curlew
skimming across the lake,
glistening branches shiver with frost
as he explains the solar system,
the structure of the earth and when
I tip-toe fearfully on its crust
his large hands hold me firm.
Together, we could walk
to the rim of the world.
All tobacco, tweed and leather smell,
a man who knows where he is going.
The sun darkens to total eclipse.
Birds go to roost, dogs keen,
shadows are hiding, day becomes night
but he explains that things will be put right
and I believed him, on that Sunday afternoon.

Pacific in the Midlands

The boy pressed
the conch
to his ear
to hear
sea-sounds
break the shore.

Eyes closed
he could see
blue depths and
corallaceous things,
sea otters search
for abalone
acrobatic seals,
fearful shapes
of sharks.

He laid it in his
treasure-chest to
glow iridescent rays
dispersing shadows.
In the misty midland town
he heard faint cries
of sea-birds as the
rain fell down.

GLOBULAR FRUIT

Jenny O'Donovan

I bought a pomegranate.
Collins Dictionary calls them
'Many-chambered, sub-tropical globular fruit.'
This one was not rosy-skinned yet
But as the weeks had passed
It had begun to glow.
At first I thought I would eat it myself:
I like the taste and the burst of juice around the seed.
The pomegranate sat in the bowl with apples, bananas and clementines
Knowing well that it was different.
I thought I would keep it for Síofra
But days went by and the date of her coming
Came and went.

Síofra did not come.
One evening, I took the pomegranate from the bowl
Cut it in slices through the tough, rosy skin
And ate it in minutes.
Now I have neither pomegranate nor daughter.

MIRACLES

Louise Tyner

Who would want miracles out of a book
When they're all around if you care to look?
There's a brilliant dandelion just over here,
Its creator a consummate engineer.
The many-rayed face soaks up the sun,
Then closes up tight—the magic's begun—
It opens a perfect ethereal sphere
Of tiniest parachutes—seeds poised to fly
As the very first breeze takes them floating by
In such myriads—many are sure to succeed
So that all good gardeners call it a weed.

Consider the hen, my own little hen
Who lays me an egg for my tea; and then
The cock crows! It's at dawn that he crows
And wakes the world as everyone knows.
He struts the yard with high burnished tail
And scarlet cockscomb—a show-off male—
But after that he doesn't do much,
It's my hen goes broody and lays her clutch
Of beautiful eggs. What is it that makes
Her keep them warm for as long as it takes
Fluffy chicks to emerge—peep out from her wings—
Where she keeps them safe from all harmful things?
Who wants to read of miracles then
When here in the yard is my little brown hen?

When you go fishing is it your wish
To pit your wits against that of the fish?
The beautiful fish clad in silver and gold:
The streamlined shape, the tales I am told—
What the journey for home-coming salmon entails,
The friendship of dolphins, the singing of whales;

That our own brown trout are the loughs' great wealth.
With my extra lung I can see for myself.
So who would choose torture from cruel hook
When Lough Corrib is there if you swim deep and look.

Have you looked at an in-calf cow 'head-on'?
You'll find before calving she's broad as she's long
At first I was worried—perhaps the vet for this cow?
'No this is normal—he's not wanted now,
For she carries a load, a calf fully fashioned.
Expertly packed, protected and cushioned.
She'll find a quiet spot far from prying eyes
She might drop her calf there before you arise.'
Next day she was slim with the calf at her side
Strong on the special milk mother supplied.

Who would want miracles out of a book
When they're all around if you care to look.

MEMORIES OF THE THEATRE

Louise Tyner

What took me from Radiography at the Children's Hospital to the Gate Theatre is all extremely vague. I think it was amateur dramatics in connection with the Unitarian Church in Stephen's Green that made me want to do more, and my mother knew the Moores who put me in touch with the Gate Theatre school under Hilton Edwards and Micheal MacLiammoir. When some of my mother's friends told her she shouldn't allow me to join a company run by two homosexuals she replied, 'And why not? I think she'll be safer there than anywhere else!' More power to her, I thought, and 'powerful' it certainly was. It meant working in hospital every morning (it had always been a part-time job) and going on to the Gate Theatre in the afternoon, and the evening as well if we were required for crowd-work, or sometimes a small speaking part. 'That's what they ran the school for,' said one friend, 'they get you to pay them, for the small parts, instead of the other way round!' However, it was a start, and how I loved every minute of it. My memory of watching my first professional dress rehearsal is still crystal clear.

It was Eugene O'Neill's *Mourning Becomes Electra* and the rehearsal went on into the early hours of the morning. I can't remember our crowd-work, but I sat fascinated in the darkened auditorium watching Hilton produce and the cast struggling with costumes and new scenery, stopped time and time again as Hilton modified his lighting or bellowed for Michael to come from the faraway scene-dock to alter or add to the scenery onstage, which Michael had created. Then Coralie Carmichael in a wonderful long clinging green velvet dress stopping in mid-speech to say: 'Hilton, I can't act in this bloody awful dress!' How Hilton comforted her, always showing his great patience with every problem: 'It looks magnificent, darling—we'll just get it lifted a bit there, and then you won't trip'. The sheer dedication of all, to go on until they got it right, be it almost up to the time when the first-night audience would begin to arrive—the show went on to the best of their ability. It was an atmosphere so different from that in which I'd lived up till then—where people counted their working hours, got regular meals and enough sleep, in hospital, in school, even in my very rational home.

There was now nothing I wanted to do more than theatre-work; but at that time I hadn't realised that the theatre was so crowded and that the real problem was finding employment. There were three or four people competing for every job, but I was happy in my ignorance for the time being.

A lot of crowd-work came our way in *Peer Gynt*, a wonderful play with music that I loved, especially Aase's death scene, which I watched from the wings every night with tears in my eyes. I had learned Solveig's beautiful song some time before, but could never hit the soft top G with which it finished—just sheer nerves, they crippled me. Soon I was given the small maid's part in Shaw's *Pygmalion* and was thrilled to bits—my first professional part—and all were very complimentary about it. But my stage voice was very underdeveloped and Hilton said, 'Louise, just shout and that will be just right!' Then one day Dr Collis arrived with his play about the Dublin slums called *Marrowbone Lane* and found me sitting in the auditorium, and recognised me as the Children's Hospital radiographer. He was one of the consultants to Harcourt Street and had taken a great interest in my 'doings' there, and straight away offered me a small part in his play. Nepotism? I suppose so, but I was so delighted to play a Nursing Sister in the short hospital scene that I didn't think about it, and I don't think Hilton or anyone else held it against me.

Every afternoon when possible Coralie Carmichael or Meriel Moore (whom my mother knew and who had been helpful in getting me into the school in the first place) would give us classes between their own rehearsals. They would set us speeches and show us how to break them up, then learn them and perform movements. But I think it was the actual performances with Hilton's help that taught me most, and anyway I think I was a 'natural'. My main difficulty throughout my theatre days was this poor memory of mine, never properly exercised since exam times, that made learning my lines such a struggle, and was, in the end, to defeat me.

Some people can learn their lines independently of the movements that are only given at rehearsal. I really needed the moves before I learned the lines and to practise them together until they became solid. We often didn't get the time to do it this way, and I could seldom make the most of longer parts in which I was just getting good by the time the play was due to come off! I remember taking comfort from watching Betty Chancellor rehearsing a speech into which Hilton had just put new moves. Time and time again she tried to match them together and failed, and Hilton would watch and say 'Try it again, darling', until suddenly she got it, and never lost it again.

Meanwhile I was 'burning the candle at both ends', and got sinusitis so badly that I had to have a very painful operation on my nose. There was no penicillin in those days. I realised I couldn't do both hospital and theatre. I had no difficulty in deciding which to give up—the theatre had become my life.

The first year had flown away, and I spent the second year also at The Gate School, ostensibly under-studying Coralie and Meriel. It was my own suggestion, to justify staying on in the school, which was a 'bit of a cod' on my part as I never paid any real attention to how Coralie and Meriel did those speeches I had picked out; but it kept me going, hoping Hilton would know my potential. He did but broke it to me gently that there was no place for me in the company at that time. They were going on tour, and one of the students who had started at the same time as I did had married his stage manager, and Michael's niece, Sally Travers, would be touring with them. These two would be sharing any small parts, leaving nothing for me. I could see the point and retired gracefully, but asked his advice. He suggested that Anew MacMaster, Michael's brother-in-law, might have an opening for me as one of his company who had been on tour with him was retiring, and they very kindly arranged an audition with him for me. But I was soon to find out that Anew, or Mac as his company knew him, was difficult to pin down, and I remember my irritation after travelling out to the far end of Howth and with difficulty finding his cottage at the very back of beyond, only to find he wasn't there. But I kept on trying and finally did meet him at the Gate Theatre and did a speech, or read a part—I can't remember now, and he was kind but vague and said I could join his company 'probably next month'—he would get in touch with me. I was delighted and thought it was all fixed, but the lady never left and kept on doing another part for him, and I was told again and again, 'Next month, darling, for sure.' It was agony. Because now I had no hospital job, and couldn't look for theatre work if I was joining his company the next month. Believe it or not, this went on for six months. It seemed an age to me with nothing to do, so finally I wrote and told him that I would not wait any longer and was going to look for other work.

I've wondered ever since should I have gone on waiting? The actress I was replacing did actually leave the company in the autumn and rang up to ask me why I had given up. I was feeling low and victimised when my sister-in-law came to stay and wrote the following poem for me:

ODE TO A SAUSAGE *by Raydene Hutton*

An actor called Anew McMaster
Wanted Louise and he asked her
To go on a tour
Beginning May four
But alas on that date he just passed her.

This same stupid Anew McMaster
Told Charlotte Louise he had cast her
For parts small and great
That might lead to the Gate
If she worked just a little bit faster.

Miss Hutton who doubted McMaster
Consulted with W.A.M.A.* who grasped her
Just in time from Anew
Whose contracts—too true—
Were worth less than an old-fashioned plaster!

This made me laugh so much in the middle of disaster that I've carried it in my handbag ever since.

---

* *An actors' trade union.*

REQUIESCAT

Oscar Wilde

Tread lightly, she is near,
   Under the snow,
Speak gently, she can hear
   The daisies grow.

All her bright golden hair
   Tarnished with rust,
She that was young and fair
   Fallen to dust.

Lily-like, white as snow,
   She hardly knew
She was a woman, so
   Sweetly she grew.

Coffin-board, heavy stone,
   Lie on her breast,
I vex my heart alone,
   She is at rest.

Peace, Peace, she cannot hear
   Lyre or sonnet,
All my life's buried here,
   Heap earth upon it.

GLENDALOUGH

Christine Fuchs Gumppenberg

Again you see the tower and the ruins
the withered shelter of the monks
and feel yourself entangled
as companion of their past

The gentle winds proclaim their gaiety
and chiselled stones confess belief
yet burdened haunted with the grief
of all the solitude in which they're cast

Here and yonder the brethren's prayers
still echoing from heaven
their fates retained and sown
for our future's bud next spring

A NORMAN SIMILE

Seamus Heaney

To be marvellously yourself like the river water
Gerald of Wales says runs in Arklow harbour
Even at high tide when you'd expect salt water.

TWO POEMS

Hugh Maxton

WAKING
in memory of my father, died November 1960

Someone is breathing in the room
apart from me. It is my father;
I recognise the hiss of his nostrils
closing, closing... It is late;
he is doing Milltown work,
we can use the extra money.
That stub in his hand is a rent book
high as a bible, thin as his widow.
Below it, in the shadow, I imagine
the soft metal of his heart
(a gold cog, slipping) finally burred,
refusing to bite. For my life
I cannot picture him; details
melt into light. The angle
of his nose, the slight furrow
of moustache escape me. All I have
is that sound fathered in darkness
carrying a reek of tobacco-y linen,
the taste of his lip.
    He rustles
like a curtain. Outside it is six a.m.
A sudden fleet of cars passes
drowning my breath for about the length
of a funeral. This has gone on ten years.

Cloud

Invisible mountain.
White eye of the self.
Look at the screen
regard my death.

In the harbour mouth
a blacknecked glebe.
On the mountain
invisible cloud.

And from day to day.
A psychology of
exploded moments
falls.

It is true
the blacknecked glebe
fishes quite
like no other.

It is true
the species
manifests no
little identity.

A language
without agreement.
Voice and limb
blown.

Eye hanging a fob.
Invisible mountain
in the harbourmouth.
Regard my death.

TWO POEMS

John Millington Synge

I'VE THIRTY MONTHS

I've thirty months, and that's my pride,
Before my age's a double score,
Though many lively men have died
At twenty-nine or little more.

I've left a long and famous set
behind some seven years or three,
But there are millions I'd forget
Will have their laugh at passing me.

25, IX, 1908

A CURSE
To a sister of an enemy of the author's who disapproved of 'The Playboy'

Lord, confound this surly sister,
Blight her brow with blotch and blister,
Cramp her larynx, lung, and liver,
In her guts a galling give her.

Let her live to earn her dinners
In Mountjoy with seedy sinners:
Lord, this judgment quickly bring
And I'm Your Servant, J.M. Synge.

A LETTER FROM REDCROSS

Ludwig Wittgenstein

Austrian philosopher Ludwig Wittgenstein spent several months in Wicklow in 1948, staying with a family in Redcross, an experience he described in a letter to his sister Helene:

The country here would not have so many attractions for me if the colours here were not often so wonderful. I think it must be to do with the atmosphere, for not only the grass, but also the sky, the sea and even everything that is brown are all magnificent.—I feel a good deal better here than in Cambridge.

WICKLOW

Charlotte Grace O'Brien

O ye Wicklow mountains! 'Golden Spears' of story!
Are your old chiefs forgotten? Are they gone?
Here where fleet-footed once they bounded on,
Followed by their sweet-mouthed hounds—their glory—
In the 'Glen of the thrushes', hot from the chase and gory,
Sweet-mouthed, deep-chested, faithful Brán and Sgéolan.

Erin! Thy children love, and love for ever,
With that abiding love that cannot die,
Thy cloudland, thy mountains, thine ocean, and thy sky,
Thy meadowed valleys green, thy sea-like river,
Can we tear them from our hearts? Can we sever
Those bonds? Ah! never, never—till we die.

ON DEBORAH PERKINS OF THE COUNTY OF WICKLOW

Anon.

Some sing ye of Venus the goddess
Some chant ye of rills, and of fountains;
   But the theme of such praise,
   As my fancy can raise,
Is a wench of the Wicklow mountains.

Mount Ida they surely surpass,
With the Wood-nymphs' recess, and their lurkings;
   O! 'tis there that I play
   And wanton all day,
With little black Deborah Perkins.

King Solomon, he had nine hundred, at least,
To humour his taste, with their smirkings;
   But not one of 'em all,
   When she led up a ball,
Cou'd foot it like Deborah Perkins.

The fair Cleopatra, Anthony lov'd,
But, by heaven, I'd give him his jerkings;
   If that he was here
   And shou'd think to compare
That trollop, with Deborah Perkins.

Bacchus he priz'd Ariadne the sweet,
But I wish we were now at the firkins;
   I'd make him reel off,
   In contemptible scoff,
While I toasted plump Deborah Perkins.

Might I have all the girls at command,
That boast of the Dresden, or markings;
   I'd rather feed goats,
   And play with the coats
Of cherry-cheek'd Deborah Perkins.

A fig for the eclogues of Maro,
Or Ovid's fantastical workings;
   If I haven't their letters,
   I sing of their betters,
When I touch up young Deborah Perkins.

CONTRIBUTORS

FERGUS ALLEN was born in London but grew up in Ireland, attending Quaker schools in Dublin and Waterford. 'Wall of Death, Bray' comes from his first collection, *The Brown Parrots of Providencia* (Faber and Faber, 1993). A second has since followed, *Who Goes There?*

JONAH BARRINGTON (?1760–1834) was born in Knapton, County Laois. He was MP for Tuam and then Clogher, and was knighted in 1807. From 1815 he lived mostly in France to avoid his numerous creditors, and is best remembered for his *Personal Sketches and Recollections*, which appeared between 1827 and 1832. The 'first patriot' he refers to in the extract published here is Henry Grattan, who kept a house in Tinnahinch.

SEBASTIAN BARRY was born in Dublin in 1955. His numerous plays include *Prayers of Sherkin, Boss Grady's Boys, The Only True History of Lizzie Finn* and *The Steward of Christendom*. He has also published novels and collections of poetry, and lives in Greystones.

SAMUEL BECKETT (1906–1989) won the Nobel Prize for Literature in 1969. His novels and plays include *Murphy, Watt, Molloy, Malone Dies, The Unnamable, Waiting for Godot, Endgame, Krapp's Last Tape* and *All That Fall*, many of them originally written in French. His work abounds in references to Wicklow, a region he knew intimately from his earliest years.

WILLIAM BLAKE (1757–1827) was believed by Yeats, on slender evidence, to be of Irish stock. His visionary epic poem *Jerusalem* was written and etched between 1804 and 1820.

SYLVIA BOWE is a short-story writer living in Dunlavin, where she organizes the annual Dunlavin Arts Festival.

ALMA BRAYDEN is an artist and member of the Bray Writers' Centre. She lives in Sandycove.

BREANDÁN BREATHNACH was the author of many books on Irish traditional music.

EDWARD BYRNE (1847–1899) was the editor of *The Freeman's Journal* and a confidante of Charles Stewart Parnell's. His *Parnell: A Memoir* appeared in 1898.

J.F.BYRNE was the original of Cranly in Joyce's *A Portrait of the Artist as a Young Man*, and lived at Leopold Bloom's address, 7 Eccles Street. His *Silent Years*, a memoir, appeared in 1953.

MILES BYRNE was born in County Wexford in 1780, and fought in the rebellion of 1798. He later became a *chef de bataillon* in the French army, and published his memoirs in three volumes. He died in 1862.

ETHNA CARBERY was the pseudonym of Anna MacManus (1866–1902), the author of 'Roddy McCorley' and many other poems and ballads.

AUSTIN CLARKE (1896–1974) was born in Stoneybatter, and published 18 volumes of poetry, from the verse drama *The Vengeance of Fionn* in 1917 to his *Collected Poems* of 1974. He adapted techniques from Gaelic and classical verse, and was also a noted satirist. 'In the Rocky Glen' comes from his 1968 collection, *The Echo at Coole*.

HARRY CLIFTON was born in Dublin in 1952. His collections of poetry, all from Gallery Press, are *The Walls of Carthage, Office of the Salt Merchant, Comparative Lives, The Liberal Cage, Night Train through the Brenner*, in addition to a *Selected Poems, The Desert Route*. He now lives in Paris.

CARMEN CULLEN is an English teacher, and the author of *Sky of Kites* (Kestrel Books, 1997). She lives in Bray.

LUKE CULLEN (1793–1859) was a pioneering historian of 1798.

DONALD DAVIE (1922–1995) was the foremost English poet-critic of his generation. His *Collected Poems* are published by Carcanet. He taught at Trinity College Dublin in the 1950s, during which time he wrote *Purity of Diction in English Verse* and *Articulate Energy*, as well as many poems on Irish themes.

PATRICK DEELEY is from County Galway, and has published three collections of poetry, *Intimate Strangers, Names for Love* and *Turane: The Hidden Village*, all with Dedalus Press.

WILLIAM DRENNAN (1754–1820) was a Belfast-born United Irishman and poet. He founded the Belfast Academical Institution and coined the phrase 'emerald isle' in his poem 'When Erin First Rose'. 'Glendalloch' dates from 1802.

NINETTE DE VALOIS was born Edris Stannus in Baltiboys in 1898, and is a great-granddaughter of Elizabeth Smith. An internationally renowned dancer and choreographer, she founded the company that became the Royal Ballet in 1956. *Come Dance With Me*, a volume of memoirs, appeared the following year.

PAUL DURCAN was born in Mayo in 1944 and is one of Ireland's best-known poets. His many books include *O Westport in the Light of Asia Minor, Teresa's Bar, The Berlin Wall Café, Crazy About Women* and *Christmas Day*. His poem reproduced here commemorates Cearbhall Ó Dálaigh, who was born in Bray.

JOHN H. EDGE'S *An Irish Utopia: A Story of a Phase of the Land Problem* was published in 1906.

CLEMENCY EMMET lives in Kilpedder.

ANNE FITZGERALD lives in Dun Laoghaire. She is a member of the Bray Writers' Centre and has published poetry in *Books Ireland* and *The Cork Literary Review*, and broadcast her work on Anna Livia FM.

F.R. FALKINER's 'Greystones Rocks' appears in *Dublin Verses, by Members of Trinity College*, published in 1895.

CHRISTINE FUCHS GUMPPENBERG lives in Germany.

SYLVESTER GAFFNEY's ballad, 'The Battle of Baltinglass,' appeared in 1950.

GERALD OF WALES's observations on bestiality and genetic mutations in twelfth-century Wicklow can be found in *The History and Topography of Ireland*. A Welsh-Norman cleric also known as Giraldus Cambrensis, he lived from *c.* 1146 to 1223.

MARK GRANIER has been a runner-up in the Patrick Kavanagh Award, and has published his poetry widely in newspapers and journals.

ANNA MARIA HALL (1800–1881) and SAMUEL CARTER HALL (1880–1889) published their *Ireland, Its Scenery, Character &c.* in 1842.

MICHAEL HAMBURGER was born in Berlin in 1924, and is a prolific poet and translator. 'Irish Questions' comes from his *Collected Poems 1941–1994* (Anvil).

WILLIAM HANBIDGE (1813–1909) was born in Tinnahinch in the Glen of Imaal. *The Memories of William Hanbidge* were written in 1906 and published in 1939. The author's punctuation is reproduced here without alteration.

SHANE HARRISON was born in Dublin in 1955. He lives in Bray, where he works as a graphic designer. He has published a collection of short stories, *Blues Before Dawn* (Poolbeg, 1992).

SEAMUS HEANEY was born in County Derry in 1939, and won the Nobel Prize for Literature in 1995. He is the author of nine collections of poetry and three collections of critical essays, and is the editor or co-editor of several anthologies. His strong Wicklow connections can be seen in *Field Work* and *The Spirit Level*. The poem 'A Norman Simile', included here, is uncollected.

JOSEPH HOLT (?1759–1826) was a prosperous tenant farmer in Rathdrum at the outbreak of the 1798 rising. He threw in his lot with rebels after the burning of his farm by Crown forces, and became one of the most active of all the United Irish military leaders. He was transported to Australia but later returned, and wrote his *History* or autobiography in 1818.

BIDDY JENKINSON is the author of several collections of poetry, including *Báisteadh Gintlí, Uiscí Beatha* and *Dán na hUidhre*. She lives in Glenmalure.

NEIL JORDAN is the author of a collection of stories, *Night in Tunisia*, and three novels, *The Past, The Dream of a Beast* and *Sunrise with Sea Monster*. He is also a film director: his films include *Mona Lisa, The Crying Game, Michael Collins* and *The Butcher Boy*.

WESTON ST JOHN JOYCE's *The Neighbourhood of Dublin* was published in 1912.

COLUM KENNY's *Standing on Bray Head hoping it might be so* was published by Kestrel Books in 1995.

THOMAS KINSELLA was born in Dublin but now lives in County Wicklow. His *Collected Poems 1956–1994* appeared from Oxford in 1996; his most recent publication is *The Pen Shop* (1997).

MARY LAVIN (1912–1996) was born in Massachusetts, but lived in Ireland from the age of ten, and was the author of many volumes of short stories.

NICOLA LINDSAY is the author of *Lines of Thought* (Kestrel Books, 1997).

J.F. LYDON is a Professor Emeritus in the Department of Medieval History, Trinity College, Dublin.

AIDAN MATHEWS was born in Dublin in 1956. His many books include *Windfalls* and *Minding Ruth* (poetry) and *Museli at Midnight* and *Lipstick on the Host* (fiction).

HUGH MAXTON was born near Aughrim. He is the author of numerous books of poetry, including *The Noise of the Fields, Jubilee for Renegades, At the Protestant Museum* and *The Engraved Passion*. He has also translated the poetry of Agnes Nemes Nagy, and published a memoir, *Waking*, with Lagan Press in 1997. Under his other name, W.J. McCormack, he is also the author of a biography of John Millington Synge.

PATRICK JOSEPH MCCALL (1861–1919) was a founding member of the National Literary Society and the author of *Songs of Erin, Irish Fireside Songs* and many other volumes.

ROY MCFADDEN was born in Belfast in 1921. He co-edited the influential magazine, *Rann*. 'Enniskerry' comes from his 1945 collection, *Flowers for a Lady*. His *Collected Poems 1943–1995* are published by Lagan Press.

LIZ MCMANUS is Democratic Left TD for Wicklow and the author of a novel, *Acts of Subversion* (Poolbeg, 1991).

James Mc Neice lives in Bray.

J.B. MALONE devised the Wicklow Way, and published several books on rambling, including *The Open Road* (1950), *Walking in Wicklow* (1964) and *The Complete Wicklow Way* (1988).

ÁINE MILLER was born in Cork and won the Patrick Kavanagh Award for a poetry collection subsequently published as *Goldfish in a Baby Bath* in 1992. She has won several other prizes, and lives in Dublin.

JOHN MONTAGUE was born in Brooklyn, N.Y., in 1929, and now lives in County Cork. His *Collected Poems* appeared from Gallery in 1995. He currently holds the Ireland Chair of Poetry.

THOMAS MOORE (1779–1852) was born in Aungier Street, Dublin, and was Ireland's best-selling poet of the nineteenth century. 'The Meeting of the Waters' is one of his *Irish Melodies*, poems based on the airs collected by Edward Bunting.

RICHARD MURPHY was born in County Galway in 1927. His many books of poetry include *Sailing to an Island*, *The Battle of Aughrim*, *High Island* and *New Selected Poems*. 'Roof-Tree' appears in *The Price of Stone*, and dates from a time when the poet lived on the shores of Lough Dan.

EILIS NÍ DHUIBHNE is the author of *Blood and Water* (1988), a collection of short stories, and *The Bray House* (1990), a novel.

CHARLOTTE GRACE O'BRIEN (1845–1901) was born in Cahirmoyle. 'Wicklow' comes from her 1886 collection, *Lyrics*.

JENNY O'DONOVAN lives in Bray.

DENNIS O'DRISCOLL was born in Thurles in 1954, and has published five collections of poetry, *Kist*, *Hidden Extras*, *Long Story Short*, *The Bottom Line* and most recently *Quality Time*. He is also one of Ireland's most widely-published critics.

SEAN O'FAOLAIN (1900–1991) was born in Cork, and was the author of many volumes of short stories. He was also a biographer, and edited *The Bell*. 'A Broken World' first appeared in *Midsummer Night Madness and Other Stories* (1932).

STANDISH O'GRADY (1846–1928) was a Gaelic scholar, and the author of *Early Bardic Literature, Ireland* and *History of Ireland: The Heroic Period*, as well as many other books.

PHIL O'KEEFFE was born in the Liberties in 1928. She has written children's stories and poetry and two volumes of memoirs, *Down Cobbled Street* and *Standing at the Crossroads*, both published by Brandon.

JEROME O'LOUGHLIN was born in Tralee, but now lives in Greystones. He is a retired schoolteacher.

SÉAMAS Ó MAITIÚ is a teacher and lecturer in local history, and one of the authors of *Ballyknockan: A Wicklow Stonecutters' Village* (Woodfield Press, 1997).

DIARMAID Ó MUIRITHE's 'The Words We Use' is well known to readers of *The Irish Times*.

MARIE O'NOLAN is a member of the Bray Writers' Centre. She has won several prizes for her work, and has published a volume of short stories, *Tales of a long dry summer* (Cairn Publishing, 1997).

BARRY O'REILLY is an archeologist and architectural historian, and one of the authors of *Ballyknockan: A Wicklow Stonecutters' Village* (Woodfield Press, 1997).

CAITRÍONA O'REILLY is from Wicklow. She has published poetry and criticism in many journals, including *The Irish Times, Verse, Thumbscrew, P.N. Review, Metre, Poetry Ireland Review* and *Books Ireland*. She has also edited *College Green*.

FRIEDHELM RATHJEN is the author of numerous books including *Samuel Beckett & Seine Fahrräder* (Häusser, 1996), a study of the bicycle in Beckett, and the editor of *In Principle Beckett is Joyce* (Split Pea Press, 1994). His poem in this anthology arises from his cycling the Irish Tour de France route in the Spring of 1998.

GEORGE FRANCIS SAVAGE-ARMSTRONG's *Stories of Wicklow* was published in 1892.

SIR WALTER SCOTT (1771–1832), author of the Waverley novels, was one of the most widely read writers of the nineteenth century. He visited Ireland briefly in 1825.

DAVE SMITH's *Selected Poems* were published by Bloodaxe in 1992. He lives in Louisiana.

ELIZABETH SMITH (1797–1885) was born in Edinburgh but spent most of her life at Baltiboys House, near Blessington. Her journal gives a vivid picture of mid-nineteenth-century Irish life, including the famine years, and is published as *The Wicklow World of Elizabeth Smith 1840–1850* (eds Dermot James and Séamas Ó Maitiú, The Woodfield Press, 1996).

JIMMY SMULLEN's ballad 'The Men of Thirty-Six' records Wicklow's victory in the 1936 All-Ireland Junior Football Championship. It is reprinted from Jim Brophy's history of the GAA in Wicklow, *The Leather's Echo* (1984).

JOHN MILLINGTON SYNGE (1871–1909) was born in Rathfarnham to a clerical family with strong Ballinaclash connections. He was educated at Trinity College, Dublin, and the Sorbonne, where he studied Old Irish.

A meeting with Yeats in Paris persuaded him that his future lay in Ireland. While staying in a Wicklow hotel, he reputedly listened to the conversation beneath through a chink in the floorboards. His ear for lively dialogue is demonstrated in his plays, three of which (*The Shadow of the Glen*, *The Tinker's Wedding* and *The Well of the Saints*) are set in Wicklow. Also of note is the collection of essays, *In Wicklow and West Kerry*. His early death was caused by Hodgkin's disease.

W.M. THACKERAY (1811–1863) wrote *Vanity Fair* and many other novels. His encounter with an ancestor of the present editor's, as described here, took place in 1842.

MARY TIGHE (1772–1810) was a descendant of the first earl of Clarendon, and the author of *Psyche: or the Legend of Love*. She lived at Rossana, near Ashford.

BILL TINLEY grew up in Manor Kilbride. A recipient of the Patrick Kavanagh Award, he has published his work in numerous journals, including *Stand, The Irish Times, Agenda, The Sunday Tribune* and *The Literary Review*. He currently lives and works in Maynooth.

THE CHEVALIER DE LA TOCNAYE was an eighteenth-century Breton royalist who fled France after the revolution. His *Promenade d'un français dans l'Irlande*, describing a walking tour around Ireland, was published in 1795.

LOUISE TYNER has worked as a radiologist and in theatre, and lives in Ashford.

DEREK WALCOTT won the Nobel Prize for literature in 1992. His *Omeros*, partly set in Wicklow, appeared in 1990.

DAVID WHEATLEY won the Rooney Prize with his first collection of poetry, *Thirst* (Gallery Press, 1997). He is an editor of *Metre*, and lives in Bray.

OSCAR WILDE (1854–1900) often summered at Esplanade Terrace in Bray with his brother Willie and sister Isola. The death of the latter, aged 8, in 1867 inspired his elegy 'Requiescat'. Wilde inherited the Bray properties on the death of his father in 1876, and went on to achieve celebrity as the author of *The Importance of Being Earnest, The Picture of Dorian Grey*, and many other works.

SHEILA WINGFIELD (1906–1992) was born in Hampshire and lived at Powerscourt House, Enniskerry, for many years. Her *Collected Poems* appeared in 1983.

LUDWIG WITTGENSTEIN (1889–1951) is one of the great modern philosophers, and the author of *Tractatus Logico-Philosophicus* and

Philosophical Investigations. He spent several months in Redcross in 1948, subsisting largely on a diet of charcoal biscuits, his biographer Ray Monk records, and would walk to Arklow to replenish his stock when he ran out.

W.B. YEATS (1865–1939) is Ireland's greatest poet, and was awarded the Nobel Prize for Literature in 1923. 'Sun and Stream at Glendalough' was written in 1932.

ACKNOWLEDGEMENTS

Every effort has been made to acquire all the permissions needed, and the publisher would be glad to hear from any copyright-holders not acknowledged here. Copyright material remains the property of individual authors or their estates. Grateful acknowledgement is therefore made to made to all the authors who have individually given their permission for their work to be included in *Stream and Gliding Sun*, and the following:

FERGUS ALLEN: to Faber and Faber for 'Wall of Death, Bray' from *The Brown Parrots of Providencia* (1993). SEBASTIAN BARRY: to Methuen for an extract from *The Stewart of Christendom* (1997). SAMUEL BECKETT: to John Calder for an extract from *Mercier and Camier* (1974). AUSTIN CLARKE: to R. Dardis Clarke, 21 Pleasants Street, Dublin 8, for 'In the Rocky Glen'. HARRY CLIFTON: to Gallery Press for 'Winter at Glenmacnass' from *The Liberal Cage* (1998). DONALD DAVIE: to Carcanet Press for 'The Waterfall at Powerscourt' and 'The Priory of St Saviour, Glendalough' from *Collected Poems* (1990). NINETTE DE VALOIS: to David Higham Associates for an extract from *Come Dance With Me* (Dance Books, 1973). PAUL DURCAN: for 'Lament for Cearbhall Ó Dálaigh' from *A Snail in My Prime* (Harvill, 1993). GERALD OF WALES: to Penguin Books for an extract from *The History and Topography of Ireland*, translated by John O'Meara (1982). MICHAEL HAMBURGER: to Anvil Press for an extract from 'Irish Questions' from *Collected Poems* (1995). Seamus Heaney: to Faber and Faber for 'Saint Kevin and the Blackbird' from *The Spirit Level* (1996). BIDDY JENKINSON: To Coiscéim for 'Cuairt and Chláraitheora ar Ghleann Dá Loch' and to the author for 'The Destruction of Poetic Habitat'. COLUM KENNY: To Kestrel Books for an extract from *Standing on Bray Head hoping it might be so* (1995). MARY LAVIN: To Town House for an extract from 'At Sallygap' from *The Stories of Mary Lavin, Volume Two* (Constable, 1977). J.B. MALONE: To O'Brien Press for an extract from *The Complete Wicklow Way* (1988). ROY MCFADDEN: To Lagan Press for 'Enniskerry' from *Collected Poems 1943–1995* (1996). AIDAN MATHEWS: for 'Returning to Kilcoole'. HUGH MAXTON: to Dedalus Press for 'Waking', 'Cloud' and 'Yeats at Glendalough', from *The Engraved Passion: New and Selected Poems 1970–1991* (1991) and to Lagan Press for extracts from *Waking* (1997). JOHN MONTAGUE: to Gallery Press for 'Luggala' from *Collected Poems*

(1995). RICHARD MURPHY: for 'Roof-tree'. EILIS NÍ DHUIBHNE: to Attic Press and Cork University Press for an extract from *The Bray House* (1990). DENNIS O'DRISCOLL: to Anvil Press for 'Poulaphouca Reservoir' from *Long Story Short* (1993). SEAN O'FAOLAIN: to Constable and Co. for an extract from 'A Broken World' from *Midsummer Madness and Other Stories* (Penguin Books, 1982). PHIL O'KEEFFE: to Brandon/Mount Eagle for an extract from *Standing at the Crossroads* (1997). SÉAMAS Ó MAITIÚ and BARRY O'REILLY: to Woodfield Press for an extract from *Ballyknockan: A Wicklow Stonecutters' Village* (1997). DEREK WALCOTT: to Faber and Faber for an extract from *Omeros* (1990). DAVID WHEATLEY: to Gallery Press for 'A Skimming Stone, Lough Bray' from *Thirst* (1997). SHEILA WINGFIELD: to Enitharmon Press for 'Elegy in a Country Church' from *Collected Poems 1938–1983* (1983). W.B. YEATS: to A.P. Watt for 'Stream and Sun at Glendalough'.

Finally, I would like to thank Dennis O'Driscoll, Bill McCormack and Michael Kelleher for more leads than can be easily listed here; and also a special word of thanks to Patrick Healy for Adam Duff O'Toole.